TRUCKING COMPANY

The Ultimate Guide to Start and Build your Successful Trucking Business Startup.

Be your own boss, Increase your income and set yourself up for success

TABLE OF CONTENTS

Introduction

A person interested in making money in the trucking industry should acquire as much knowledge as possible. If they don't have a background in the industry, they may work together with a person who has the experience because valuable insider knowledge could save you monetary and legal problems.

Trucking is one of the most lucrative businesses for startups because it's possible to start the business with one truck. The trucking industry offers very important transportation services to various industries; hence it has a long lifespan.

The initial cost of setting up a trucking business may be high. Still, with a great business plan, it is easier to secure both investors and money lending institutions' cooperation. It is prudent to start small, especially if you are not relying on your savings, and then you may expand your company as your sales grow.

In America, trucking is one of the fastest-growing industries based on the high number of trucking companies being registered and the great number of people employed at trucking companies. Quite a few trucking companies are also small-scale, and this should encourage you to start your own business.

Many factors influence a successful trucking company, but the key factor is drivers. The industry has historically faced a shortage of drivers, and in this era of millennials, it is even worse.

This book will provide you with all you need to know about the trucking business and how to start your own trucking company.

It aims to equip you with the expected and unexpected things that you're likely to encounter.

Chapter 1: THE ENTREPRENEURIAL

MINDSET FOR TRUCKING BUSINESS

The various underlying factors that you need to consider when starting your trucking business will be clearly outlined.

The main goal of starting any business is to make money that turns into profits. There are other benefits to starting a business that you'll get to enjoy. The economy is experiencing a tremendous growth rate. This means that there is a big opportunity for smart people to launch their own successful businesses. One of the most profitable industries is trucking. The trucking industry is responsible for the movement of items across the country. It is a very competitive field. You might want to first learn as much as you can about the industry before you set up your own trucking company, or else you risk losing valuable time, energy, and money.

Most people tend to think that all trucking companies are similar, but that is not the case. You first need to decide precisely what role your company will fulfill.

It is a great thing that you are thinking of starting your own Trucking business and taking charge of your life. However, before you take the plunge, you need to know to note that starting and running a business is not for everyone. According to a report by the Global Entrepreneurship Monitor (GEM), close to 14% of the US adult population (over 25 million Americans) are starting or running new businesses. Unfortunately, data from the Bureau of Labor Statistics show that more than half of all new businesses fail within before their fifth birthday.

Why this huge rate of failure? While there are many reasons why a new business might fail, it mostly boils down to the business owner's mindset. If you want your business venture to be successful, you need to learn how to think like an entrepreneur. Without an entrepreneurial mindset, your business might not even live to see its first birthday.

If you observe the world's most successful entrepreneurs, you will notice that they all have a similar mindset in their approach to challenges, attitudes towards risks and mistakes, learning, and decision making.

Successful entrepreneurs do not sit and wait for things to happen. Instead, they are always taking action, creating their own opportunities, and looking for ways to remain relevant. Whereas others see challenges as setbacks, entrepreneurs see them as opportunities. They are constantly trying to learn and improve themselves. They are attentive to their environment and are quick to identify and take advantage of business opportunities.

This mindset and approach to life are what sets apart successful entrepreneurs from everyone else. It is what keeps them moving forward, even in situations where giving up seems to be the logical thing to do. If you do not want your business venture to be part of the half that goes belly up before its fifth year, you must learn to think like an entrepreneur before you embark on the entrepreneurial journey.

Some people are born with an entrepreneurial mindset. Being an entrepreneur comes easily to them. Fortunately, it is a trait that can be learned, assimilated, imbibed, and put to practice by those not born with it. You can teach yourself to think like a successful entrepreneur by following any of the tips down below.

Find Your Passion

All successful entrepreneurs are extremely passionate about what they do. Their business consumes their whole lives, and they are willing to make big sacrifices. For instance, Facebook founder Mark Zuckerberg decided to drop out of Harvard to bring his idea of a social network to life. Similarly, Jeff Bezos quit a very lucrative job on Wall Street to start Amazon. The passion for what they are doing keeps entrepreneurs going, even when things do not seem to be going their way.

To become a successful entrepreneur, you need to learn how to follow your passion. Don't get into business just because you want to make money or because an entrepreneur's life looks glamorous. It is not. There will be lots of difficulties and challenges and thoughts of quitting. In these moments, it is your passion that will keep you going.

Get Comfortable With Risk

Being an entrepreneur is synonymous with risk. Starting a business is a risky affair. You never know whether it will work or not until you do it. For instance, after making millions from PayPal's sale, tech billionaire Elon Musk put all his money into his passion project, SpaceX. He was left with no money, yet SpaceX was blowing through money without making any. At some point, he was so broke that he had to survive on loans from his friends. But he kept at it. He was soon back on his feet quickly after signing a multibillion-dollar deal with NASA, which also saved his company from collapse.

Would you be willing to take such a huge risk? Successful entrepreneurs are not afraid of taking risks. They have a high tolerance for risk. Similarly, if you want to be a successful entrepreneur, you must constantly step out of your comfort zone. However, this does not mean that you should take risks blindly. Instead, you should weigh the risk, assess its potential benefits, and put measures to minimize the risk. Most importantly, do not be afraid of failing. Failure is merely another opportunity to learn and improve.

Adopt A Goal-Oriented Attitude

Successful entrepreneurs know that they are responsible for the outcomes of their lives and their businesses. They know that success is not a matter of chance – it is their sole responsibility. Therefore, they don't live life aimlessly. They set goals for themselves, whether in life or business, and make sure every action they take is geared towards achieving those goals.

To be a successful entrepreneur, you need to adopt the same mindset. Have goals for every sphere of your life. Before you start your business, determine what goals you want to achieve, when, and the steps you need to take to get there. This will provide you with direction and ensure you don't waste your time and energy on things that are not beneficial to you or your business.

Learn To View Challenges As Opportunities

Most people try as much as possible to avoid challenges. When they encounter a difficulty, they either give up or change course. Successful entrepreneur understand that challenges are a part of life. When they encounter challenges, they don't back down or give up. Instead, they look for ways to overcome the challenges, and in so doing, discover opportunities most people would miss.

As an entrepreneur, you have to be ready for and comfortable with facing challenges and problems. Starting and running your business is not going to be easy. You will encounter endless obstacles and setbacks. Your attitude towards these obstacles is what will determine whether you will be successful or not.

Learn To Think Strategically

To start and run a business, you need to become a master strategist. You need to spot opportunities and quickly determine the best way to take advantage of them. You need to learn how to attract prospects, turn them into paying clients, and keep them coming back. You need to set your business apart from the competition, give it an edge, and remain relevant. All these require constant planning, reviewing your results, and optimizing your strategy.

Understand The Ecosystem

Businesses do not operate in a vacuum. Other businesses surround them, customers, and governmental regulations, all of which impact your business. To be a successful entrepreneur, you need to understand your business and the ecosystem in which it operates, or else you might be caught flat-footed by unanticipated change. For instance, what if the government passes a new policy that directly affects the future of your business.

Do you take the time to consider what such policies mean for your business? As an entrepreneur, you must observe the entire ecosystem in which you operate and watch out for any changes that might impact your business.

Be Driven By Your Vision

Successful entrepreneurs do not act blindly nor in haste. They have a vision for themselves and their business. They know where they are going and what they are trying to achieve. They dedicate their lives to following this vision and do away with anything that might be distracting them from it. All their resources–time, money, and effort–are expended in line with this vision. Most importantly, this vision keeps them on the straight and narrow even in the face of challenges.

If you want to become successful in business, you need to develop a vision for yourself. Why did you start your business? Where do you see yourself in five or ten years? From there, everything you do in business should take you closer to this vision. When things get tough, remembering why you started will push you to overcome the obstacles you face. Have a vision. Plan for it. Execute it.

Be Disciplined

You need to prioritize your business and forget everything else that does not contribute to its success. You need to put in a lot of time and effort to work when you would rather be doing something else. Maintaining the level of effort, energy, mental stamina, and drive needed to succeed a business requires the utmost discipline. You can compare being in business to going to the gym every morning. Sometimes, the thought of leaving your comfortable bed to go work out is not appealing. Sometimes, it is too cold weather, feeling tired, etc. But if you want to meet your fitness goals, you have to remain disciplined, stick to the plan, and go to the gym anyway. Similar to what is expected of an entrepreneur.

Chapter 2: TRUCKING COMPANIES AND LOGISTIC

Here are the main classifications of the trucking companies:

For-hire truckload carriers

These trucks essentially haul other companies' freight. Many companies need logistic support and supply chain management. Companies contract for-hire truckload carriers to transport their products. The business model is ever-changing because it is based on the freight demands of the companies you work with and contract terms. When the contract reaches maturity, the client – in this case, the company – may allow other trucking companies to bid on it. And so, the nature and availability of freight are subject to change, and one of the measures of protecting yourself against loss is having multiple customers.

Private trucks

If you have a company that produces a particular product, you might want to distribute your own product instead of contracting out trucking companies. Private trucks are thus used to transport freight that belongs to the parent company.

Whenever private fleets are unable to meet their freight demands, they may contract out other truck companies.

Household Movers

People are relocating every day, and they need to bring their stuff along. Establishing a household carrier company will facilitate the movement of peoples' belongings. Considering the high percentage of people who relocate because of family, financial, or even work-related reasons, this is an especially lucrative field.

Inter-modal

In this model, trucks' only function is carrying the freight to and from the railroad yard. This is how it works: a truck carries a load to the rail yard, the load is transported by rail, and finally, another truck carries off the load from the rail yard to its destination.

Trucking logistics involves the management of operations to ensure all activities of the business run smoothly. This includes planning accordingly, the organization of goods, and having the proper documentation, among many others. Proper logistics management ensures efficient and timely services to customers.

Areas of business logistics that benefit the trucking business

1.   **Warehousing** - This is the core area of trucking companies. It holds a great amount of the company's assets and production. A

warehouse benefits your trucking business in providing space for the storage of goods before they're dispatched. Lack of storage space will render your trucking business ineffective, therefore it should be a top priority. Logistic solutions showing goods for delivery and disposal should be accurately and clearly assigned.

2.   **Efficient back office** – This is where planning, communication, and documentation are managed. An office helps ensure that your schedules are well planned so that you're able to tell what deliveries are to be made and what needs to be dispatched. This in turn aids in giving the customers accurate information about the exact date and time they can pick up their freight.

Logistics perspective on business

The two types of transportation logistics that are used in the trucking businesses are as follows:

Outbound logistics – Goods that are distributed from a company to their customer.

Inbound logistics – Goods received from a third-party source, such as raw materials for production or stock.

In both outbound and inbound logistics, the main requirements include the scheduled Estimated Time of Arrival (ETA) and official documents such as Delivery Receipts (DR), Invoices, Bill of Landing (BOL) and Certificate of Compliance.

Warehousing is an essential part of logistics management. For goods to be stored properly, there must be adequate space available at specific times. To ensure space, it's essential for a purchase order (PO) to include delivery schedules to avoid going over capacity.

Data management is important in the trucking business. Data software stores client information, manages delivery schedules, determines truck maintenance times, locates cargo, and organizes other complicated operational services of a trucking business.

Importance of logistics solutions for trucking companies

1-   **Meeting customers' needs** - To meet customers' needs, trucking companies must operate with flexibility and swiftness. Owning a transportation logistics software will equip your trucking business to deliver an efficient operation of service to the stakeholders. It will also help your trucking business act by the greater standard requirement for a professional trucking company.

2-   **Easing the distribution process** - The storage of cargo and the safe delivery to various destinations are monitored by the personnel, bringing down costs in the distribution process.

3-   **Maintaining schedules** - Delivery schedules are processed smoothly, therefore striking a balance between the available trucks and truck drivers. By doing so, trucking companies' timely and safe delivery of goods improves their services and profitability over time.

4-   **Smooth operations** - Employing logistic solutions provides an organized smooth-running process of your human resources, routine plans, fleet availability, maintenance, and data management needed to keep your operation agile, straightforward and methodical.

5-   **Reduces cost of manpower** - The trucking business is highly operational without using a lot of manpower. Affordable technology is available to keep track of day-to-day business operations.

6-   **Order fulfillment** – Logistics enables delivery of goods as per customers' detailed specifications thereby ensuring that customer requests are fulfilled.

Outsourcing and third-party (3PL) logistics

Outsourcing in the trucking business is a way of distributing work for a cheaper cost. Outsourcing and third-party logistics involve other companies' services to act by the requirement of a client.

It comes in the form of third-party warehousing or by leasing space from another warehouse. The most popular way of outsourcing in this industry is by using additional trucks that may be required for the delivery of goods or equipment.

It's important to note that most companies outsource their trucking needs when special trucks are required for one time or occasional delivery of certain goods. For instance, a textile manufacturing company that operates regular delivery trucks may need to relocate or sell one of their machines requiring a trailer to transport the equipment.

Licensing, importation, and exportation

As part of logistics, licensing will play an integral part to ensure that you act by the legal requirements of each commodity.

Whether your trucking business falls under importation or exportation, trucking services should have the right documents to manage their services. You will be responsible for licensing since it depends on the company or the shipper but never on a third-party trucking company.

Logistics computerization

In the trucking industry, the computerization of dispatching time and route has made things easier. This has been made possible by using the GPRS, which has enabled companies to track down their trucks and their current status.

It has added security to truck drivers, the company, and the goods as well. This GPRS automation has rendered an easier task in the trucking world as it provides a wireless solution for monitoring the handling and transportation of goods and managing the delivery schedules and trucking services based on the clients' needs.

The availability of this kind of safety innovation has also attracted insurance companies to take part in trucking. As one of the most in-demand businesses, trucking companies capitalize on the growing improvement of modernization and automation.

With the aid of modern transportation logistics solutions, they're able to minimize costs while improving their trucking services' efficiency.

Therefore, now is the best time for you to start your trucking business.

Chapter 3: BUSINESS AND FINANCIAL PLAN

A trucking company, just like any other business, requires a business plan, which is the mirror of the business. It's a clear reflection of the business, which is not only useful for personal purposes, but it's vital for seeking prospective partners, investors or financial assistance from banks.

Your business plan should contain a clear mapped out plan on what the company does, what it stands for, what sets it apart from its competitors, future predictions of the company's financial position, and how you plan to achieve its goals have set out for yourself.

Contrary to popular belief, drawing up a business plan is quite easy. However, you will need to dedicate time and effort to carry out the needed research for various business plan sections. While there are different kinds of business plans, depending on the nature of the business you intend to start, there are some key elements that are found in most business plans.

The Executive Summary

This is usually the first part of a business plan. The executive summary provides a quick overview of what is contained in the rest of the business plan. It outlines your business, what you do, who you are targeting, and some key financial highlights.

The executive summary aims to give readers without a lot of time (such as potential investors) the big picture of your business. Ideally, the executive summary should be able to stand on its own. It should be very clear and concise, highlighting all the key aspects of your business, without going into too much detail. You can think of it as a one-page business plan. Some investors will only ask for your executive summary, rather than the whole business plan.

If they like the information presented in the executive summary, they might then ask for something to shed more light on your business, such as a pitch presentation, a complete business plan, or more detailed financial information. Therefore, you need to make sure that your executive summary is intriguing and compelling. However, if your business does not require financing or partnerships and you are only writing a business plan for your own purposes, you can leave out the executive summary.

Even though the executive summary is the first chapter of your business plan, it is recommended that you write it last, after you have written the rest of the business plan. This way, you will have a clear idea of what is in the rest of the business plan. Remember, the executive summary is, just as it sounds, a summary of your business plan.

Ideally, your executive summary should be about one page in length. Below are some of the things that the executive summary should cover:

Problem Summary: An overview of the problem you are trying to solve for your customers. This is basically a justification for why your business needs to exist.

Solution Summary: An overview of what your business does, its products and services, and how they are different from what is in the market.

Target Market: A brief overview of the market segment you are targeting.

Competition: An overview of your key competition.

Marketing Plan: A summary of how you intend to reach your customers.

Current Financial State: A brief overview of your company's current financial status.

Financial Forecasts: A brief overview of the financial targets you intend to hit in the next 6 months, 1 year, or 2 years.

Financing Needed: If your business plan aims to secure funding, give a brief overview of the amount of money you need. If you aren't trying to secure funding, leave out this part.

Why Us: A brief overview of the people involved in running the business and why they are the right people to run this business.

The Opportunity

This is the first chapter of a business plan. This is where you go into detail about the problem you are trying to solve, how you are solving it, the market segment you are targeting, how your product fits into the market, who your competition is and how you will deal with them so on. This chapter should contain the following sections:

The Problem Worth Solving: In this section, you will define your business's problem for its customers. Here, you will need to answer questions such as what your customers' primary pain point is? What are the existing solutions for this pain point? Why do you feel that the existing solutions are not effective? To properly define the problem, you will need to go out there and talk to potential customers. What you think is their greatest problem might actually not be a problem. The only way to validate your assumptions is to talk to them.

The Solution: In this section, you should go into how you intend to solve the problem you identified above. What are your products or services? How do they solve the problem? Why are they better at solving the problem compared to what is in the market?

Target Market: After defining the problem and describing your solution, the next thing is to explain who you intend to sell to. Here, avoid the temptation to describe your target market as everyone. Just because you have a product that everyone can potentially use doesn't mean that everyone will be willing to buy it. Identify the group of people for whom the problem you are trying to solve is a real pain point. Having a good idea of who your target market is will help you come up with the right sales processes and marketing campaigns.

Market Research: Don't just stop at describing who your target market is. Go a step further and research how big the market is and the different segments within that market. This will help you determine if the market is big enough to support your business's success.

Market Trends: In this section, you will describe the notable changes that are happening in your target market. Are there any significant changes in the needs and preferences of your potential customers? Is there a new market segment starting to gain interest in the kind of products or services you are offering? How do you intend to take advantage of these changes to give your business an edge?

Market Growth: This section will explain the growth your target market has undergone over the last couple of years. Is it growing or shrinking? If the market is growing, this is a good sign, since it shows that there is an increasing demand for solutions to the problem you are trying to solve. If the market is shrinking, this is not a very encouraging sign, though it is still possible to succeed in such a market. However, you will need to understand that you are swimming against the current. To find out the kind of growth happening in your target market, you will need to carry out a lot of research.

Competition: In this section, you will describe who your key competitors are. To determine who your competitors are, you should think of the various ways through which your customers currently solve the problem you are trying to solve. Here, even businesses that do not seem to be direct competitors could still compete with you. For instance, if you are launching a beer brand, you might assume that your only competition is other beer brands and alcoholic drinks. However, if someone is sitting in a restaurant waiting for some- one, a question like this might go through their mind: should I drink a beer or soda? Because both your beer and soda are solving the same problem (the customer needs something to drink), they are both in competition, albeit indirectly. Apart from describing your competition, you should also describe which competitive advantages you have to gain a chunk of the market share. Do you have access to new technology that your competitors do not? Do you have some intellectual property rights that make your product or service superior?

Execution

This is the second chapter of your business plan. This is where you will go into the details about how you will make your business work. In this chapter, you will cover things such as how you will sell and market your products, how your business will operate, how you will measure success, and so on. This chapter will include the following sections:

Marketing Plan: Here, you are going to describe the strategies that you will employ to reach your target market, as well as how you intend to position your business and your products and services in the market. Your chosen strategies will depend on your ideal customer. For instance, if your ideal customer spends more time on Instagram than Facebook, then part of your marketing plan will include Instagram marketing. Your marketing plan should include details such as your pricing plan, and the reason why you decided to price your products that way, your positioning statement, which explains how you will position your products and company to differentiate yourself in the market, and your promotion strategies, including the reasons why these strategies are the best suited for your target customers.

Sales Plan: This will describe how you will get your customers to buy your products and services. Mention any sales channels and processes you have in place, the people who will be in charge of selling your products, and the place where you will sell your products.

Operations: This section details how your business will operate. Here, you will need to describe things such as the people or companies that will supply you with the raw materials you require for production, the locations and facilities where your products will be produced, and how you will get the customers' products. If you are not manufacturing your own products, describe how you will get the products, whether through partnering with wholesalers or through dropshipping.

You should also describe all matters to do with your inventory, such as how much inventory you intend to maintain, where this inventory will be stored, how you will monitor and track inventory, and how you will deal with unexpected spikes in demand busy seasons. If you have some technology that will play a key role in your business operation, describe it and how it works.

The point here is to show the reader that you have a pretty clear idea of how your business will work and your supply chain and that you have solid plans to deal with potential uncertainties. If you are writing the business plan for yourself, the operations plan will help you make key decisions about your business, such as reducing costs, how to price your products, how to plan your break-even point, and so on.

Milestones And Metrics: For a useful plan, you need to break it into steps that you need to follow while implementing the plan. In this section, you will describe the steps you need to take, the dates before which the steps need to be completed, and the people responsible for each of these steps. You will also describe the key metrics that you will use to monitor and keep track of how your business is growing. Examples of metrics that you might want to monitor include the number of leads generated, sales, website visitors or any other metric that will give you a good idea of how your business is growing. The milestones and metrics section does not need to be overly long. The point is to make it clear what steps need to be taken to make your business successful.

Key Assumptions And Risks: Here, you will describe the key assumptions you have made that are crucial for the success of your business, both favorable and unfavorable. For instance, if your business's success depends heavily on Instagram marketing, you are assuming that Instagram will always be a great platform for marketing. If Instagram were to shut down a few months down the line, this would pose a huge threat to your business. The good thing with knowing your key assumptions and risks is that it allows you to prepare. If you know your key assumptions, you will focus on proving if they are correct. The aim is to minimize assumptions and therefore remove any uncertainties from your business. Similarly, when you know the risks you might face, you will start developing contingencies before these risks become actual problems.

The Company

This is the third chapter of your business plan. This chapter provides an overview of your company, including the structure and the people involved with running it. If you are writing the business plan for your own use, you have the option of leaving out this chapter. It is usually the shortest chapter in the business plan, and consists of the following sections:

Company Overview: In this section, you are going to describe the ownership of the company, its legal structure (sole proprietorship, incorporated company, limited partnership, or general partnership), a brief history of the company and why it was founded, as well as its location. You will also include information such as the mission and vision, the company's values, any intellectual property held by the company, the nature of the business, the industry in which the company is operating, and your business objectives.

The Team: In this section, you will give a list of all the key members involved in the running of the business, a brief bio of these team members, as well as an explanation as to why these people are the right people for these roles. Most businesses succeed or fail depending on the those who are tasked with running them. Moreover, investors will want to know the company's people and their qualifications before putting money into the business. Even if you are writing the business plan for your own use, this section can help you discover any team's oversight tasked with running the business.

Financial Plan

This is the final chapter of your business plan. This chapter is crucial because running a successful business involves paying close attention to your income and expenditure. Having a solid financial plan will help you make key decisions like deciding when you can purchase new equipment, bring in new employees, expand the business, and so on. If you are trying to secure funding from investors or financiers, a good financial plan will also help you determine how much money you need to get your business off the ground, which will, in turn, help you determine how much money to borrow.

Sales Forecast: In this section, you are going to provide projections or estimates about the number of sales you expect to make over the next two or three years. You don't have to go into too much detail at this point. Just provide a high-level overview of how much you expect to sell. If your business has multiple products or services, you should provide projections for each product or service separately.

Personnel Plan: In this section, you will go into the details of employee salaries. If you are starting a small business, you can create a list of all the people you intend to hire and the amount of money you will pay each of them every month. For a big company, this might not be feasible. What needs to be done in this case is a break-down of the personnel plan by departments, such as "sales," "finance" and "IT." You are also going to include the employee burden in this section. Employee burden refers to other costs that come with having employees on your payroll other than salary. This might include things such as insurance and taxes.

Profit And Loss Statement: Also referred to as an income statement, this document brings together all your numbers and helps you determine whether you are making or losing money. The income statement includes all your revenue sources within a given period (extracted from your sales forecast) and your expenses over the same period (personnel costs, production costs, and all other expected expenses). The income statement gives a bottom line by subtracting the expenses from the revenue and determining whether you will be making profits or incurring losses.

Cash Flow Statement: The cash flow statement is almost similar to the income statement, and sometimes even gets confused with the income statement. Like the income statement, the cash flow statement consists of a list of your revenue and expenses.

However, there is one key difference between the two. Whereas the income statement will include revenue from all sales within a certain period and all expenses from the same period, the cash flow statement also considers when your company collects revenue and pays out its expenses. As a result, it is a great tool for keeping track of the amount of cash that the business has at hand at a certain time. Unlike the income statement, the cash flow statement does not calculate profit and loss. By keeping track of the amount of cash you have at hand, the cash flow statement helps you determine when you have surplus money or low amounts of cash and might need to borrow money to keep your business running. Since your business is still new and money has not yet started flowing, you should create a projected cash flow statement for the next twelve months.

Balance Sheet: This is a financial statement that gives you a look into your company's financial health. The balance sheet consists of a list of all the assets owned by your business (equity) and a list of what you owe . Subtracting the total liabilities from total assets will help you determine how much your business is worth.

Trucking Start-up cost

This section clearly outlines your trucking company's financial position

based on capital which is the startup cost and the anticipated regular monthly expenses of running your business. There could never be an exact cost for starting a trucking business as the prices could vary based on your location, goods you haul, and business size. Using America as an example, the following should guide you as you carry out your personal research to ensure that you don't leave anything out.

a)   Buying the trucks

First, you need to determine the trucks you want to buy and the price you will get them. It's wise for a start-up company to go for a second-hand truck cab which could cost as little as 20,000 or so, instead of spending around $113,000 to upwards of $180,000 on a new truck cab. This of course isn't even considering the trailer's cost, which can cost another $30,000-$75,000 depending on what you get. If this option proves to be difficult for you, there is still an option of seeking companies that can allow you to pay in installments.

b)   Registration

Once you have bought your truck, you need to have it registered with the department of motor vehicles or any other regulatory agencies in your operation area. You will spend at least $500 to be able to get this done.

c)   Business Licenses and Permits

You will need to get a business license and permits that will allow you to run your trucking business, drive past your border and carry specific goods with specific weights. It is difficult trying to find the right website that will help in obtaining permits. Some websites list all of the requirements needed according to your particular state of operation. These sites will also guide you on the DOT requirements as well as how to obtain a CDL.

d)   Insurance

This business requires that you carry insurance. Transporting valuable goods carries the risk of damage, loss or other unforeseen risks. You must also insure all drivers who will be on the road.

Insurance in the business of trucking is not a one-off expense rather it will be a regular expense. Allocate an annual budget of $1,000 to $2,000 if you are the owner-operator on lease and $8,000 to $12,000 plus the owner-operator under your own authority.

e)   Office / Parking space

As a start-up, you could operate from your home or rent office space. Include this cost if it's the latter. However, you must get a secure parking space for your truck, which will cost you some money. This will be a regular monthly expense.

f)   Website and load board

It's important to set up a website as you start your business. You could do it yourself with the help of online programs or seek a website developer's services. Either way, you'll most likely incur a cost of between $100 and $200 to get this done. Setting up the load board and accessing customers will also incur extra costs, which you must include in your calculations.

g)   Marketing and promotion

Include the cost of marketing and promoting your trucking business which have to research for estimates. Get quotes for the cost of creating the company logo, branding your truck with the name of your company and logo, creating and printing brochures, business cards, and other materials for promoting your company. Depending on the area you want to reach, estimate at least $500 for all of these expenses. Marketing and promotion will fall under regular monthly expenses as well.

h)   Staffing

As you start, you can be the driver, accountant, and receptionist at the same time, but as your company grows, there will be so much to do which you will eventually find overwhelming. You will have to share and delegate various tasks to ensure your business runs smoothly. Consider the cost of hiring staff and paying salaries, wages, insurance, etc. which will all be regular expenses.

i)   Maintenance costs

This is an unforeseen cost that can happen anytime the truck breaks down or requires routine maintenance. Make sure that you budget for this expense in your regular monthly expenses.

j)   Miscellaneous

This is extra money that may come in handy in case of a business emergency or any other need that may arise.

Therefore, the total cost of starting a trucking business is at least $ 10,000 for a single truck and $50,000 plus for having several trucks.

By now, the important question on your mind is, how do I make money in this business? Simply put, you make money by transporting goods for your customers either directly or through freight brokers. For your business to realize profits, several factors have to be considered.

1. Finding the right market niche

You should consider the right market niche by going after the markets avoided by large carriers. This means focusing on hauling goods such as food grade liquids, livestock, fresh produce, and meat. Taking fresh produce and meat as an example, one reduces competition, maintains work throughout the year, and counteracts recessions.

You'll be guaranteed consistency since fresh produce and meat are regularly transported all over the country. Access to local produce markets, farms, or directly from wholesalers provides stability and good profitability.

2. Charging the right rate

You should consider having the right rates to make profits. This involves finding out how much the brokers pay, getting to a load board, getting more loads headed towards the same direction, knowing how much the brokers pay the shippers and knowing the rates for specific lanes. As you do all these, keep in mind that your rates should bring you good profits while covering all your operating costs.

3. Establish your operation costs

For you to make a profit, it's important to know your costs of operation. This is achieved by determining the fixed costs and the variable costs. Fixed costs remain constant in your business whether your trucks are on the road or parked. Examples include permits, insurance, truck payments etc. Variable costs are derived from the number of miles driven by the trucks which obviously vary depending on the distance covered.

4. Minimal use of brokers and load boards

Working directly with your customer enables the establishment of a reliable relationship. This can be made possible by offering your customer more competitive rates than those offered by brokers, while at the same time eliminating a percentage of the money that goes to the brokers. In this case, you get to keep the whole amount.

5. Running an efficient office

You can work from home for a startup if you have a computer, a printer, and access to the internet. You'll also need an accounting software and you're good to go. As your business grows you'll grow with it and get a space to rent.

The following are the benefits of starting a trucking business.

1. Independence

By starting a trucking business, you get to make your own decisions from what to haul, when to work and who to work with. You'll also have total control of your income, which could lead to financial freedom.

2. Flexibility

The trucking business offers flexibility by enabling you to make your own schedule allowing you to work when it's convenient for you. This is made possible whether you're an owner-operator or employ truck drivers. You can broker or deal directly with shippers and you don't have to be tied to one customer.

3. Profitability

Starting a trucking business enables you to be in control of the rates you charge. If you're an owner-operator, you keep the profit accrued from the business. Once you build relationships and maintain great customer service, you will be able to enjoy the generated revenue, leading to profits.

4. Variety of customers

Transportation is key to various industries; from farmers, to manufacturers, to merchants, and contractors. These industries create several market niches to choose from; including food deliveries, courier firms, private carriers and carriers for hire.

This business stands out compared to other businesses which are mostly limited to a specific industry in which to operate.

5. Availability of opportunities

Despite trucking being one of the most competitive businesses in existence, there is still room for start-ups who mostly start as owner–operators or carriers for hire. The trucking business also experiences a shortage of truck drivers hence it offers opportunities for new drivers who have obtained a CDL (Commercial Driver's License). This is not the case in other businesses where you find unhealthy competition due to market saturation.

CHAPTER 4: UNDERSTANDING TRUCKING COMPANIES

The United States Labor Department estimates that about 70% of freight is hauled by trucks. This means that the trucking industry silently plays a key role in the economy. If it were sabotaged, there would be a crisis in the supply of food, clothes, electronics, and other products.

Owning and operating a trucking company is not a bed of roses. The initial start-up cost is high and the operating and maintenance costs, and there are many logistic challenges. However, these should not discourage you. The trucking industry is virtually like any other industry; those who can adapt can make money, but those who are unfit are forced to quit.

You may rely on your contacts for business or freight brokers and shippers. The processes around freight are done carefully. The driver must have the requisite paperwork, and the freight must be recorded electronically. The driver might be the most visible person in the trucking industry, but other personnel are just as important, such as mechanics, dispatchers, safety directors, and salespeople. In cases where expensive products or irreplaceable art pieces are moved, there may be armed guards aboard the truck.

You may make your truck all-purpose or tailor it to a certain niche. For instance, some trucking businesses may focus on transporting food products, other chemicals, household property, etc. Generally, it is better to align your truck to a certain niche – opposed to swallowing every opportunity – as it promotes trust and expertise. You are much more capable of developing a relationship with your customers when you are devoted to a certain niche.

The biggest challenge for a new owner-operator is finding loads. The trucking industry is extremely competitive, and it can be difficult to find customers much more when you are new. Unavailability of consistent loads is what forces many trucking companies to close. But how should you go about finding loads?

Load boards are great, but you should think further. To be successful in the trucking industry, you need to have repeat customers; and you can only have repeat customers when you establish relationships. Getting loyal customers is an uphill task because customers are spoilt for choice. However, if you combine great pricing and quality service, you are bound to attract loyal customers.

Load Board

Also referred to as freight boards, these are online platforms that allow brokers and shippers to post loads and carriers to advertise their services. Through these boards, shippers and carriers may find each other, make a deal, and facilitate freight movement.

You can post loads, search for loads in unique criteria, and find even more services offered to both carriers and freight brokers. Here are some of the services you may find:

Load matching

Payment details

Message platforms

Shippers' and carriers' reviews

FMCSA verification

Factoring services

Mobile contact

There are both paid and freeload boards. As you can imagine, the competition on the free load boards is fierce. This may force you to lower your charges against your will to have a fighting chance. The paid load boards may have quality loads, but the competition is still high, and there is not an abundance of loads posted anyway. Overall, paid load boards are far better. New owner-operators who do not have clients usually start at the load boards.

Operating a trucking company requires lots of patience. This is because most shippers and clients take forever to pay, which might make your company susceptible to cash flow problems. One of the major tricks around this problem is working with a factoring company. What is the work of a factoring company? When you need cash, it comes to your aid by buying your accounts receivable at a discount. Thus, getting urgent money for things – such as fuel and maintenance – and, more importantly, taking on more business growth opportunities, is much easier.

Many load boards facilitate the access to freight bill factoring that gives carriers a chance to cash their freight bill as soon as they wish. Some factors offer fuel advances by providing funds for fuel when you pick up the load. Fuel advances are typically expensive. They are best suited for freights which have a huge profit margin.

Relying on load boards alone is a tedious and futile business practice. Once you get a client, you should establish a relationship with them by offering value-added products/services or getting their contacts and constantly asking for opportunities. You may also decide to go around your area of operation and look for new businesses that need carriers or seek to oust other carriers by offering better rates to clients.

Three Important Things before Submitting a Bid:

1.   Determine your MPG

Find out how many miles per gallon your truck can get.

2.   Determine the mileage cost

Find out the total miles that the contract requires you to travel.

3.   Determine daily cost

Divide the total miles by the average miles you can complete in a day, and then multiply the number of days it will take to finish the job by the amount you expect to make daily.

Choose your structure

Many different structures are used to operate businesses. These structures describe how the business is run, including the model of the business itself. They also includes information about how each structure is likely to grow, what you can do to scale, and more.

You must pick the right structure for your business. Not only will this help with the model of your business, but it also contributes to the legality factor. Below, you will find information about all of the different legal structures you may consider when developing and running your business.

Sole Proprietorship

A sole proprietorship is the type of structure used by individuals or married couples in business alone. These tend to be the most commonly developed business structures, as they are simple to create and operate. There are fewer legal controls in these structures in general, allowing greater flexibility when it comes to operation. There are also fewer taxes involved. The primary downside to this structure is that you carry all liability personally.

Home Business

Some businesses, typically sole proprietorship businesses, may be run as what is known as a "home business." This means that the business is run from the individual's home. Businesses like this have a broad range in what activities are fulfilled. They also still have a certain amount of legal requirements to ensure that protection standards are met. If you are running a home business online, the number of legal requirements you have are low, if any. If you are running a home business where clients will be coming into your home for any reason, you need to look into your local legal requirements. Most require you to have a business/home inspection done, have your space licensed, and purchase insurance to protect your clients and yourself. Certain requirements will likely need to be met to ensure the safety of the general public.

General Partnership

General partnerships include two or more partners together who have agreed to each contribute to the business. They typically contribute through money, labor, or their skills. The two or more individuals are typically not in a marital relationship when they are in a general partnership legal structure. Each person is included in profits, losses, and general management over the business itself in this structure. They typically carry equal partnership rights, meaning they are equally able to receive benefits and receive liability for the business. Typically, general partnerships are drafted up with a formal partnership agreement written as a contract between the partners.

Limited Partnership

Limited partnerships are like general partnerships, except that one or more of the structure partners are considered to be limited. This means that the general partners are responsible for managing the business itself and are involved in sharing in the profits and losses that the business realizes. Limited partners will share profits, but will be protected against any losses based on how much they have invested in the company. A limited partner will not typically become involved in day-to-day operations for the business. These structures are generally required by law to be filed with your local government.

Limited Liability Partnership (LLP)

Most professionals use this structure. It is essentially the same as a general partnership, except that partners will not have personal liability should another partner be negligent in their business. These are really common structures in lawyers and accountant offices. The individuals are typically at higher risk of negligence and partners want to be protected from someone else's potential mistakes.

Limited Liability Limited Partnership (LLLP)

This limited liability limited partnership is typically the same as a limited liability partnership, except there are statements in the certificate that indicate the limited partnership. These structures are also known to be useful in protecting general partners as well as limited partners.

Corporation

Corporations carry a far more complex system compared to sole proprietorships or partnerships. Corporations become their own independent identity outside of the individual or partners, and therefore the corporation carries its own privileges, rights, and liabilities. There are typically many tax and financial benefits that come with running a corporation. However, they may be offset by other things that business owners need to consider, such as the increased cost of licensing fees, or the decreased amount of personal control that the individual has over their company.

Non-Profit Corporation

A corporation that registers as a non-profit, is one that is structured exactly like a corporation. However, the goal is more in the business's interest than in the profit it can create. These are typically used to serve public interest, such as charities or otherwise. If you run a non-profit corporation that also intends to raise donations from public donors, you will likely need to register for a Charity Program as per your local laws. This will provide you with a charity number, legitimizing your charity and further protecting yourself and your donors and [customers] from potential fraud.

Limited Liability Company (LLC)

Limited liability companies are comprised of one or more individuals. These companies include a special written agreement that details the LLC organization, assigns interests, includes any provisions for management, and how profits and losses are distributed. A company that registers as an LLC is generally capable of carrying out any for-profit business activities, other than banking or insurance.

Hearing how many different structures exist can be daunting. You must choose the proper structure for your business. This ensures that you can run it accordingly, that it is legally structured in a way that protects you and your partners (if applicable) to the maximum extent. The structure serves the best interests of your company.

Choosing what structure you need is not as hard as it may seem. In fact, it truly varies from person to person, and situation to situation. This is especially true in the circumstances of small businesses or start-ups intended to launch into the small business world.

In some cases, talking to an attorney may be the best strategy for discovering the best structure for your unique business. This ensures that your legal interests are covered and that you understand what the laws for your local area are. Remember, they do vary from place to place, meaning that you need to ensure that you are clear on what applies to you when structuring your business. This will keep you, your business, and your clients safe.

Outside of the idea of talking to an attorney to get access to the best information possible, you can also consider the following. Answering the questions below will give you an idea of where you are at in your business.

How many individuals are currently involved in running your business?

If the answer is just you, or just you and your spouse, you might want to consider running a sole proprietorship. This is one of the easiest structures to form and has the ability to give you flexibility in how you run your business. If you want to limit your personal liability, you might consider registering as a Limited Liability Company.

If the answer is you and other individuals, consider looking into starting a partnership. This will enable you all to be legally accounted for and protected in your business. Be sure to work with an attorney to get this set up in the best structure for each of you. This will determine what type of partnership will best suit your business's needs and the partners involved.

If you are looking to build a business with partners and multiple employees, you might consider starting a corporation. This allows the business to become its own entity and be supported legally to mitigate any legal liability from each individual involved in running the company.

How much liability are you willing to take on?

Liability equals risk. If you are held personally liable for anything, this means you could potentially stand to lose a lot. For example, in a situation such as a sole proprietorship, you are on the line with unlimited liability. This means should anything tragic happen, you are held personally responsible and have to face any consequences as a result.

If you are running a company where the liability is seemingly low or protected, you might consider maintaining your status as a sole proprietorship. If you are a partnership, you might consider becoming limited liability partners to prevent any of you from being held responsible for the other's mistakes. Or, you might consider becoming limited liability partners to protect you to the max against any mistakes in the business in general.

Alternatively, if you don't want to hold any responsibility and you have enough individuals to form the structure, you might consider starting a corporation. This takes the personal liability load off everyone involved and ensures that you are all protected in the event of a tragic accident. In this circumstance, the corporation would take all of the risks and you, personally, would take none. This means that the corporation could lose everything, but you will likely remain safe (depending on the details of the circumstance).

What legal structure best serves your business?

Of course, you need to think about your business goals and objectives. Naturally, certain structures will serve specific goals that you may desire to achieve. For example, if you are looking to start a charity, you will likely want to register as a non-profit corporation. Alternatively, if you start a business on your own, you may want to start a sole proprietorship. That is unless you want to limit your risk, then you might consider a limited liability company. If you were going into business by yourself, you would not want to enter into any form of partnership agreement, as it would not hold up for you.

Ensuring that you choose the structure that will best serve your business now and in the future is important. While you can generally amend what you initially choose, it tends to be easiest to start in the way that is going to serve your future goals the best. That way you do not have to incur expensive legal fees later on to advance to where you desire to go.

Once you have considered these questions, you will likely have a strong idea of what legal structure will best serve your business. Again, if not, going to speak with a business attorney may be your best opportunity to ensure that you are structured the proper way. It is essential that you choose the proper structure, as this will protect you and set you up for success in the future of your business.

These are some of the basic requirements that you may have to fulfill before starting and operating your own trucking company:

Commercial Vehicle Operator's Registration

Business Liability Insurance

Assistant's Licenses

Driver's Licenses

Ownership Proof

ID

Fire Certificate

Certificate of Incorporation

Business Plan

Business License

Non-disclosure Agreement

Employee's Handbook

Employment Agreement

Operating Agreement

To be on the safe side, you might want to visit the United States Department of Transportation, the Federal Highway Administration, and the Federal Motor Carrier Safety Administration to check whether other legal requirements are required to set up your trucking business, especially if your niche is sensitive. For instance, moving hazardous loads might require additional certifications.

Insurance

You must take out various critical insurance cover before you are allowed to operate a trucking business. The trucking industry is very risky. It would be misguided to forgo insurance considering that some of the risks can potentially ruin your business. Additionally, most clients want to work with trucking companies that have their insurance coverage in order.

These are some of the necessary insurance coverage needed for your trucking business:

Physical Damage Coverage

Commercial Auto Liability Insurance

Bobtail Insurance

Motor Truck Cargo Insurance

Non-Owned Truck Insurance

Occupational Accident Insurance

General Insurance

Liability Insurance

Workers Compensation

Health Insurance

Medical Insurance

Overhead Expense Disability Insurance

General Liability Insurance

This is an insurance policy that safeguards your business against several claims such as bodily injury and property damage that may occur during business operations. If you get a Business Owners Policy, some insurance companies will lump both General Liability Insurance and Property Insurance together.

The General Insurance Cover safeguards your company against claims involving workplace accidents, unruly employees, and wrong delivery. Some insurance companies will require you to acquire a primary liability policy to be eligible for general liability.

Cargo Insurance

This is an insurance policy taken on the load being handled by a trucking company. This policy protects the business against loss or damage of the cargo from a road accident or fire accident. Additionally, it also covers unintentional clearance of cargo, undelivered cargo, and late delivery. In this coverage, you decide your limits that inform what your insurance company would have to pay. You may have to choose the limit of your deductible that is the cost incurred by a claimant. This policy covers the following vehicle types: tractors, cargo trucks, trailers, cement mixers, and dump trucks. This policy does not typically cover freight, including money, art, jewelry, tobacco, contraband, alcohol, and explosives.

Bodily Injury and Property Damage

The Bodily Injury policy covers against injuries and accidents that might happen in transit. The policy may be instrumental in facilitating, for example, the payment of medical bills. The Property Damage covers against property destroyed by road accidents. The policy allows you to set your limits.

Physical Damage Insurance

There are two types of physical damage insurance: comprehensive car insurance and collision insurance. The policies cover for any damage done to trailers and trucks. The two policies may be bought separately. Collision insurance covers damages arising from collisions while comprehensive car insurance covers damages from theft, fire, vandalism, and animal attack.

Excess Insurance

Sometimes, your company may find itself in circumstances that you had never thought of. This policy covers for the unexpected situations that your trucking company might find itself wedged in. This insurance policy has potential to cover for liability running into millions of dollars.

Bobtail Insurance

This policy covers when your truck is not being utilized to transport goods, such as when your truck is getting repaired.

CHAPTER 5 : FUEL CARDS

A fuel card is like a credit card, but businesses are used by businesses involved in transport and fleet management. It allows cash free purchase of fuel at gas stations. Just like normal credit cards, fuel cards involve swiping and entering a PIN by the user. Several fuel card companies offer fuel cards as per customers' needs by granting them access to a network of gas stations. Using a fuel card for your trucking company will also save you money.

Types of fuel cards

The following are the types of fuel cards offered:

1.   **International** – These are cards that can be used through third-party agreements. Customers can refuel at automatic gas pumps.

2.   **Bunkered** – This involves fuel card service providers reserving fuel at a specific gas network to offer it at a discount. The customer can save money because the fuel is at a pre-negotiated price despite the rising market price.

3.   **Retail** – Customers have the option of refueling at any gas station across the nation.

4.   **Company** – This card is used by fleets whose main operation is transportation. They're greatly affected by any changes in fuel prices.

All fuel cards being offered by fuel card services have various discounts for their business customers. Most customers compare fuel cards with credit cards. The following are the main differences between the two:

1. Fuel cards offer discounted fuel prices while credit cards do not.

2. Unlike the fuel card, the credit card comes with a greater security risk.

3. One must keep receipts of every transaction when using a credit card which is not the case with fuel cards since it's used for fuel only.

4. Fuel cards have restricted use at networks while credit cards can be used anywhere.

5. Unlike a fuel card, the credit card can't measure efficiency or filling patterns.

Most trucking companies use fuel cards. You should also consider using fuel cards in your business to aid in fuel cost management as well as fuel efficiency.

Benefits of fuel cards

The following are the benefits of fuel cards:

Service customization - Several fuel card providers have applied personalized customization. For example, one customer service employee will be assigned to serve the same company, making it easier to identify its needs.

Single invoicing – Fuel card management has eliminated the need for drivers to collect receipts or invoices for administrative handling. The fuel card companies provide a single invoice with summarized fueling history. Depending on the package, these invoices are sent weekly or monthly.

Discounted fuel price – Cost saving is a great priority for any business. Fuel card companies purchase fuel at prices lower than the stipulated retail price. This is highly beneficial to those large companies who operate a large number of vehicles in their fleet.

Easy to use – Having accessible fuel filling history and costs on a single online platform saves a lot of time and effort by minimizing the otherwise tedious steps that would have to be followed by fleet managers and accounting departments in retrieving that data. It also provides access to extra functions such as the amount of fuel consumed weekly. It also has more sophisticated systems like a database with fueling patterns and fraud alert systems which are sent by text message or email for customer convenience.

High-security – Fuel cards operate on a PIN code and chip technology which encourages drivers not to carry unnecessary cash with them and reduces risky situations while at the same time preventing activities related to fraud.

Every card is registered to an individual driver or vehicle, allowing tracking regular patterns and comparing them to averages on databases. Any abnormal activity can be spotted immediately, and relevant people are alerted via text message or mail.

More control over expenses – Company managers can monitor fuel costs and consumption costs incurred by drivers by having personalized reports. This involves having each driver's account set up separately and enabling central control. This also prevents unauthorized purchases.

Fuel card companies are divided into two groups:

Independent – Independent fuel card companies offer an array of different cards irrespective of their brand.

Branded – They are also known as bunkered. These fuel card companies provide cards that can only be used in certain gas stations in their network.

Businesses select fuel cards based on various factors such as organizational processes, consumption patterns, and its fleet.

Factors for customer consideration

Below are the factors that customers need to consider when investing in fuel cards:

Invoicing option – As discussed earlier, when operating your trucking business, you will be in a better position to determine your company's accounting system, cash flow, and other administrative activities. The fuel card company will be able to send your billing either weekly, monthly or even quarterly as per your request which is based on your needs

Availability of personalized customer service – The fuel card company should have an assigned customer service agent that handles all your queries and meets all of your business's needs.

Single network versus a range of gas station networks – Depending on your trucking company's needs, you should be able to decide whether a single network of gas stations or a gas station network is best for you.

Discount program – Every fuel card comes with the added perk of pre-negotiated discounts.

Level of security – Fuel cards don't carry high-security risks like credit cards do, offering you a better option for your business.

It's important to note that some fuel card companies provide fuel cards for free and all that is required is a certain minimum usage in a specific timeframe.

Some companies charge fees based on the payment plan and network coverage. The approximate cost of a single fuel card ranges from $7.65 to $31.87 annually.

How to purchase a fuel card

Purchasing a fuel card is a simple and fast process because you will just need to access your preferred fuel card service provider's website where you can fill in your personal information. When applying for fuel cards a customer is required to have the following information:

1. Bank account details

2. Full business details

3. Vehicle and driver's information

After filling in the form online, the rest is taken care of by the fuel card company on their end. Usually, a customer is contacted soon after the application is processed with a business package proposition that is tailored to meet the customer's needs.

You should contact the fuel card company for assistance before choosing how you want to use the fuel card since it can be an overwhelming task.

Fuel cards are just about the best way to cater to your truck or fleets fuel expenses. Here are some of the best fuel cards:

Comdata

This fuel card has nationwide coverage. This card can be accepted in 600,000 stations since it can be used as a debit card. It allows drivers to pay for fuel, tolls, and other related expenses.

The Comdata app enables users to manage funds, locate stations, and review various stations' services.

EFS

This fuel card covers both the US and Canada. The card offers discounts on other significant items like tires, auto parts, equipment, and lubricant.

Fleet One

This card covers the entire country and extends its services to Puerto Rico and Canada. This card is accepted in about 90% of fueling stations in America. The card allows users to track the expenses by showing the balance on their online platform. The card also provides discounts, reports on fuel activity, scheduling, and expenses.

Fuelman

This card focuses entirely on commercial clients. Fuelman offers two types of fuel cards: Fuelman FleetCards and Universal Cards. The Fuelman FleetCards can be used in over 50,000 sites, and they offer discounts and alerts. The Universal Cards may be used anywhere MasterCard is accepted. The Fuelman app assists users to locate the nearest station offering their services.

Wex Cards

These cards are mainly used by government affiliates and are tailored to them, but anyone else can use them. The Wex Cards help you control your budget by keeping track of your expenses.

US Bank

The US bank fuel card is tailored for truckers. Users may process fuel transactions in various stations throughout the country, offering powerful data analysis tools.

Shell

The Shell fuel card may be used for transactions in all Shell stations.

The user may be able to track their expenses.

BP

The BP fuel card is tailored for truckers. It is not only useful in facilitating fuel transactions but also reduces costs. There are various rewards and bonuses attached to the card.

ExxonMobil

ExxonMobil offers two cards. Both cards are entitled to a discount of 10 cents per gallon at ExxonMobil sites for the first six months, and then 6 cents per gallon moving on.

Arco

The ARCO fuel card may be used at over 1,500 ARCO fuel stations across the country. The card features include password controls, online statements, vehicle and mileage tracking, disabling stolen cards, and restricting the type of expenses.

CHAPTER 6 : SOFTWARE FOR TRUCKING COMPANIES

Thankfully, technological advancement has led to the creation of software that simplifies management.

Here are some of the advanced digital tools tailored for trucking companies.

ProTransport

ProTransport is sophisticated software that provides solutions in fleet management. The software brings all the aspects of management together and makes it easier for the owner/manager to track performance, make decisions, and save time.

The software integrates every feature of your business into a coordinated system. The platform has a great user interface designed for easy access to the key features.

Axon Trucking Software

This trucking software is available for businesses in the United States and Canada. The dispatch and accounting functionalities are integrated in real-time. This saves time because information is relayed as it happens, therefore as the owner or manager, you have more time to grow your business, improve service delivery, come up with new ideas and spend time with family.

Using the Axon Trucking Software, you will not need to keep whiteboards, papers, and sticky notes anymore as you can make a dispatch through the software. The software can provide field tickets, and can also integrate all your company's management applications, as well as track expenses.

TMW Systems

TMW Systems was found in 1983, and the company has upwards of 2,000 customers operating both small and large trucking companies as of today. Customers may select the management software or particular products for accounting, maintenance, or dispatch. All the functionalities of this software help in saving time and fuel and evaluating the driver's performance and the maintenance of assets.

The company's mission is to renovate the way freight moves around the world. Thanks to the incredible features that help in business intelligence, asset management, and scheduling, the software boasts an extremely high customer retention rate. Incorporating this software into your business will save you time and increase your profit.

PCS Software

This company has created management software for transportation companies for over two decades now. The software is cloud-hosted, and it provides real-time reports. The mobile App ensures that you can access the platform no matter where you are.

The PCS truckload dispatch system is both powerful and easy to deploy. It has the capability to disseminate dispatching responsibilities. The Intermodal Dispatch promotes efficiency, productivity, and generation of more income. The LTL Dispatching System has built-in management and route-optimization features which saves time and improves the income margin. The PCS Software facilitates communication between freight brokers and carriers, thus creating revenue opportunity and reducing expenses, for example, load boards.

Prophesy

Prophesy has served the trucking industry for more than twenty years. This software is capable of deploying important functionalities like accounting, communication, dispatch, load planning, safety compliance, and IFTA reporting.

Through the communication feature, you can maintain contact with both the drivers and clients, which lowers your stress levels. The software integrates into QuickBooks Accounting, Microsoft Dynamics, Sage and others, thus ensuring an optimized billing cycle. The software also helps you to stay compliant with the industry's rules and regulations. Moreover, since it is cloud-based, the reporting is done in real-time.

Having been in business for more than twenty years, the Prophesy Software has shown quality, dependability, and affordability.

ITS Dispatch

The customers of ITS Dispatch include owner-operators and freight brokers and small and mid-size carriers. The software is affiliated with the popular load board, TruckStop.com. The software facilitates the important integrations that help customers grow their business. According to the research by TruckStop.com, installing ITS Dispatch increases your rate of processing loads by 31%, grows your business by 16%, saves eighteen hours per week, and boosts profit by 12%.

ITS Dispatch allows customers to swap the ITS Dispatch logo with theirs, giving the software a custom look. The mobile App allows you to access the platform regardless of where you are, and it is crucial in facilitating communication between drivers and dispatchers.

Tailwind Transportation Software

Tailwind Transportation Software is an award-winning online software tailored for fleet, brokers, brokerages, and carriers.

Customers may choose one of the three plans: Standard, Pro, and Enterprise.

Using this software, you may fulfill compliance, paperwork, and dispatch duties without experiencing any difficulty. Setting up an account is free – no contracts or wait periods. For thirty days, you may enjoy the software's functionalities free of charge, and then decide which plan best suits you.

Tailwind helps you track all the company's essential facets in one platform, thus boosting efficiency, saving time, and increasing profit margins.

McLeod Software

McLeod serves a small fraction of the transportation industry. Its two main products are (1) the LoadMaster dispatch software and (2) the PowerBroker software. McLeod's other software helps in sales, marketing, and the measuring of fleet performance.

Benefits of a Dispatch Software

Dispatch software will have a great impact on your trucking business. Below are some of the benefits:

Management of transportation

Management software makes it possible to have absolute control over every transportation and mobile employees' processes. It allows tracking your team's location and status in the field using tools like GPS (Global Positioning System), allowing control over when and where you can dispatch your employees.

It will be improving your team's routes and consistency in the quality of services rendered to your customers.

Quick response

In the trucking business, many things can go wrong on the road. Since it's not a guarantee that things will run smoothly every day, dispatch software is crucial for spotting and tracking incidents, providing you with real-time data on your employees' location and status.

Flexibility

The more your business grows, the more complicated the dispatch process is, which could lead to errors if there is a lack of proper systems in place to prevent them.

Dispatch software solutions are designed for flexibility. They can manage scheduling and dispatching ensuring each load is delivered to the client on time. It can also be made unique to meet your specific needs.

Essential Features of a Dispatch Management Software

The following are the most important features of a dispatch management software:

GPS Tracking and Mapping

A reliable GPS tracking and mapping function is important because a dispatch software relies on tracking each employee's location and status. It gives access to real-time data, such as the current traffic conditions. Having this data makes it easier for your employees to identify the best possible routes to ensure a timely delivery of services. It also enables easy navigation through unknown areas through the integration of a map service.

Automated scheduling

A trucking business needs to automate manual tasks to enable effectiveness. A dispatch software will comfortably allow you to handle tasks that run concurrently, like monitoring business growth while tracking scheduled jobs, customers that need to be served, and available technicians.

A dispatch software makes it possible to manage your employees' schedules quickly and easily. It also enables you to assign multiple tasks in an instant. You'll be able to identify the right technician for each job. The technicians will also take less time in making repairs since the dispatch software provides them with most of the necessary information.

Mobile access

In the trucking business, drivers who are mobile employees need an accessible and convenient communication channel. Dispatch software comes with mobile apps that allow drivers to receive any necessary information and quickly respond to the office.

A two-way communication channel is established, allowing employees in the office to communicate with drivers and technicians about any arising issues. Drivers can reduce the time it would take to complete paperwork. This is possible since the mobile app enables them to control their trips and access relevant route information while automatically collecting and storing data of their progress. In turn, errors are greatly minimized.

Automated notifications

As your trucking business grows, automated notifications will come in handy since it will be difficult to keep up with all the progress as it happens in real-time.

Some of the tools offered by fuel card companies work by automatically notifying dispatchers of trips that may fail to meet their delivery schedule, spotting issues with scheduling days in advance. This information helps with proactively solving issues with a few clicks instead of trying to fix problems as they occur or after they occur.

This software also helps track each driver's performance, making it possible to identify the areas of performance that need improvement.

Convenient invoicing

The software eliminates the time-consuming process of invoicing while in the field by streamlining it and considerably minimizing the time it takes.

It can also track every expense, from equipment to labor while at the same time successfully sorting out rates and customers' discounts if there are any. When it comes to the technicians, the software enables collecting payments from credit cards, offering a convenient billing and payment system that results in customer satisfaction.

How to choose Dispatch Software

Many of the leading dispatch software comes with various features that could make it overwhelming for someone just starting their trucking company to make the right choice. How do you find the best software fit for your trucking company?

This will depend on your priorities. For a startup with a single truck or two, your decision will be based on the price. When this is the case, it eliminates some software service providers based on your budget. Your trucking company can choose a less expensive option that provides the key functions needed to operate your business.

For those with more experience, you will need to look beyond the budget to maximize the software solution's value as opposed to the cost. As a startup, it's important to know that just because there is a cheaper solution doesn't mean that it will be worth it. It might be incapable of meeting your trucking company's needs or it could be unadaptable as the business grows.

Cheap can sometimes mean expensive. If you have to change systems and start from scratch, it can ultimately be more expensive to your business. Not to mention your trucking business's losses if the initial system fails to meet the business projections.

Simultaneously, just because a software system is expensive, that doesn't guarantee that it's efficient for your business. Even the most expensive software solutions can have unreliability issues, poor support, or missing key functions needed by your trucking company.

To increase your return on investment, the following are a few questions that will assist in narrowing down your list:

What features are most important for your company?

Dispatch software comes with various features, and not all software service providers have the solutions you need since they all vary.

You need to establish the features that will be of most value to your company. By so doing, you'll be able to make several eliminations from your list of software companies. These features include integrated map services, remote monitoring, and mobile app availability among many others.

Does it offer comprehensive training?

Rigorous training programs should be offered by the software provider to enable your trucking company's employees to utilize it to the maximum extent, which will go a long way in ensuring that you benefit from the software solution.

These trainings equip the employees with the knowledge to operate the software, but it should also offer substantial support in case the need of additional features comes up in the future.

It's advisable to try the demo version of the solution and see if it's compatible with your business's needs.

How does pricing structure compare with functionality?

There are different cost structures for different software providers. It's important to determine which provider is within your budget requirements.

For example, depending on your company's size, you may or may not need to get a customizable software. You'll need to determine if the extra cost of that feature will be worth it with where your business is currently at and where it's projected to go.

CHAPTER 7: IMPORTANCE OF HIRING THE RIGHT EMPLOYEES

According to the U.S. Department of Labor, a bad hire's cost stands at about 30% of the annual salary for that position. Below are the benefits of hiring the right employee:

You will minimize the cost of the hiring process

It is a known fact that the process of hiring is very expensive. Not only does it require you to take time out of your already busy schedule but you will also spend money on job postings, skill tests, criminal background checks and much more.

Whenever you hire the wrong person, you will have to conduct the same hiring process all over again hence doubling the cost. Hiring the right employee will eliminate the need for a second hiring process as well as the added cost.

You will maximize productivity

Time is valuable hence conducting a hiring process means you and your team will leave your daily routines to review applications and conduct interviews. When you conduct several interviews every day for a few weeks, it becomes difficult to finish your other work. A fast and rigorous hiring process will allow you to get back to your work sooner and with enhanced productivity.

You will save time

Time spent reviewing applications and conducting interviews will be saved. When you spend most of your time going through the hiring process, you lose interest due to the monotony of it all.

This might cause you to miss out on the recognition of a good candidate. You will find that every resume looks about the same.

The hiring process should occur less often and further apart to enable you and your hiring team to be refreshed. Having a clear head gives you an easier time for when you have to hire again.

Saves you from potential damage

For a lot of different reasons, bad hires can hurt your company. Some could be a safety risk to customers and colleagues hence the reason for conducting criminal background checks.

A bad hire might ruin your company's reputation and jeopardize your client relations by being incompetent among so many other things. Bad hires almost always damage your business in some way. Avoiding a bad hire means you will not have to deal with any such potential damages.

You will preserve the morale of your internal teams

A good hire comes with new skills and experience to your team and brings inspiration, warmth, and togetherness to your company culture. On the other hand, a bad hire could hurt your entire team's morale by harming the work culture through a bad attitude or being a joyrider or a bully.

You will protect your image as an employer

When your company culture goes bad, the news will always spread outside. For instance, let's say your employees keep leaving because they are not happy with their jobs anymore, and they say negative things about your business.

These things will give a poor reflection of you and your company such that other people will not want to join your team. Hiring the right people, however, will always protect your reputation.

You won't let the good candidates leave

Hiring someone means having to turn down dozens of other applicants. A good number of those who have been let go are probably qualified for that position.

If you happen to get the right employee, losing the rest won't hurt as much. However, when you make a bad hire, it can be so annoying to know that you let better candidates go.

By the time you realize this most of them will probably have found other jobs or would not be so keen to come back to a place where they already faced rejection.

You don't have to train an employee who won't stick around

The entire hiring process is quite a struggle, but usually the biggest annoyance is employee onboarding. Helping new employees to blend in, training them and familiarizing them with your company's processes and policies usually takes a lot of time.

Despite how talented or adaptable the person is, the process of onboarding does not happen overnight. It could take your new hire months if not a year, depending on the position's level.

Investing all that time and effort into someone who will not be a part of your company's long-term future is the greatest blow of making a bad hire. That's not even to mention that you will also have to go through the entire onboarding process again.

The constant movement of drivers plagues the trucking industry as they seek greener pastures. This shows that a lot of drivers are not satisfied with their work environment. Regardless of these challenges, you can still fish out a great driver when taking the appropriate measures.

Here are some of the ways to ensure that you find hardworking and loyal drivers.

Pay Well

When you pay your drivers well, they are motivated to do their part extremely well. Also, they will be less tempted to commit fraud. On the whole, the industry rates are quite low. Those who can afford to pay extremely well seem to be the long-established fleets that enjoy a high income. Unless the freight rates go up, some owners cannot afford to give their drivers a decent salary.

A great method to work around this problem is to offer a flat rate and a performance-based on remuneration. This will make the driver want to work a little bit harder to secure large commissions.

Involve The Drivers

Take the time to find out the views of drivers. Sometimes working for a big company might make a driver feel like a cog in a wheel, and if anything bothered them, they would not bring it up. When you set up systems through which drivers can communicate, you show them that you value their contribution. Also, you should be a bit more intentional when devising new plans for your business. For instance, if you plan to start operations on a new route, you may want to ask about their views. When you show a driver that they are a part of the business, they will be less inclined to flee when the opportunity occurs.

Ask For Referrals

Perhaps this is the best method of hiring. Your fellow business owners are well aware of several drivers. And so, if you have an open position, you should go to them first. This way, you increase your odds of finding an experienced driver.

Colleagues are aware of what certain drivers are like, and they may guide you when you need to fill a position. There are many unhinged drivers in the trucking industry – some are flippant with work or even criminals. Bad experiences with drivers may translate into losses. Also, take care as to whom you solicit referrals. Not everyone would love to see you working with the best.

Use The Internet

As much as the referral is the best method of looking for drivers, you must understand that capable drivers lack civilian networks. You may use the Internet to reach such drivers.

There are job boards, Facebook groups, and online communities catered to drivers. And so, you may want to post your requests here and go through the responses. When you hire a driver from the Internet, it is prudent to put them on probation to see what they are really like before accepting them wholly into your business.

Another method of looking for a driver through the Internet is by organizing a contest for drivers.

Be Honest

When you are hungry for a driver, you might be tempted to sugarcoat the reality. This never works. For instance, if you lie about work hours or routes, you might cause the driver to resent you. And when enough resentment builds up, the driver will most likely runoff. When you are honest, you set the tone for conducting business. But when you lie, you might tempt your driver to lie also – if only as a way to fit into the apparent company culture. So, recruiters must resist the urge to create unrealistic expectations in the minds of drivers.

Onboarding

When you have a new hire, you should not just brief them on their tasks and send them on their way. Instead, you should practice the fine art of onboarding. This is where you inform your new hires of the rules, regulations, and procedures to assimilate well into the company. It is a chance to project the image of having a community.

As the manager or owner, you may want to have a sit-down with a new hire over lunch to orient them about the business, and afterward, the new hire should meet everyone involved in the day-to-day operations of the business.

Having a proper onboarding procedure gives the new hire a sense of belonging.

Put Driver Health First

The job itself is hectic, but you may want to show your driver that you care. You should also invest in facilities like gyms and promote healthy eating, exercising, and on-site screenings. Having healthy drivers discourages absenteeism, and your business may run without glitches.

Also, your payment packages should be inclusive of sick leaves. For instance, when a driver is sick at home, they should have the security of a salary.

Handle Problems That Drivers Raise

Besides low pay, another factor that forces drivers to quit jobs is management's failure to attend to their concerns. A great company should put the needs of its drivers first, which means their problems should be resolved as quickly and humanely as possible. When the drivers' needs are met, they feel respected and more obligated to play their part well. However, when the drivers' concerns are ignored, it usually causes a buildup of resentment which only results in driver-exodus.

The quality of the people you employ will get the job done, but they will also have an impact on company culture and the company's financial worth. Before we look at the importance, we will cover the things to consider when hiring. They are as follows:

1.   Focus on the person

Focusing on the person addresses the importance of a candidate's social intelligence, which is how well they interact with others. It basically helps employers focus on the candidate's personality instead of just meeting the job qualifications. Companies can teach new skills through training but they cannot teach on acquiring new personalities.

You could start by identifying the most important character traits you are looking for and then building a list of related questions. The interview will turn into a conversation that can reveal how they will be in terms of organizational skills, ability to be trained, transparency and humility. The personality should match the company and the job since different job functions need different personalities, which will go a long way in contributing to the company's success.

2.   The ability to learn

With the development of new technology and business processes, job responsibilities and tasks also change often. Part of the employers' evaluation should be how well and fast the candidate learns new things.

3.   How they answer probing questions

Being ready to probe further when particular responses to interview questions are given is one way of getting a view of the candidate's personality. For instance, let's say a candidate is asked about his or her reason for leaving his or her previous job.

The response the candidate gives points the reason at a manager or colleague.

This suggests that this candidate is shifting the blame to someone else.

Upon getting such a response the employer should ask more questions that could lead to the candidate pointing fingers at others whether it is the whole answer or just a part of it. Employers should take this as a warning sign if it emerges to be a pattern.

4.   Allowing them to demonstrate their skills

The entire hiring process is a test. The candidates who demonstrate transparency, humility, desire, and organizational skills will always stand out. This technique will help weed out those who do not demonstrate these qualities. This will help to avoid making big mistakes when it comes to hiring.

5.   Understand what they are really looking for

As much as every person wants to get paid, it is not the key to making the right candidates happy. You need to know what's in it for the potential candidate because satisfying an individual's motivators is the best way of retaining a good employee.

6.   Long-term growth and potential

When looking at potential employees, it is also important to factor in their potential growth. You should be able to project the employee lifecycle.

Like stated earlier, just because their skills are written on paper does not mean that they can accomplish the job at hand. Do not be under the impression that just because the candidate has the right experience, they are right for the job.

You should try to find out if they have any other skills apart from those required for the job. It is important to know if the candidate can solve problems because it will mean that they will not need to be constantly guided.

CHAPTER 8: CHARACTERISTICS OF IDEAL EMPLOYEES

Good employees are recognized through the qualities they possess. It is paramount as an employer to identify good employee's qualities since they are an asset to your company.

Retaining good employees is also quite challenging. You will want to hire good employees who will stay for a long time. Without putting the entire emphasis on personality, there are other distinct qualities to look for irrespective of the candidate's age or gender. They are as follows:

-        Ambitious

To achieve company goals or climb the corporate ladder, ambitious employees are always willing to go the extra mile. They will give their very best because they set goals and high expectations for themselves. They also strive to advance in their career. Ambition activates creative ideas, openness and a go-getter attitude, which are good for your company. Your ambitious candidate should, however, have a reasonable amount of emotional intelligence. This will ensure that he or she does not isolate most of his or her workmates.

-        Confident

As the owner in your trucking business startup, it will obviously make you happier handing a project over to a confident person instead of a doubtful person. A confident person will be willing to take on the challenge and the risks that come with it, all of which the uncertain person would shy away from. People who believe in themselves have a great outcome. If you were to let a candidate interact directly with a client, they would be impressed by the confident person, encouraging them to continue the business relationship.

-        Humble

People do not like those who brag about their achievements. The preferable candidate should be capable of proving himself/herself through their hard and admirable work as opposed to just words. Arrogant employees do not belong in a productive workplace.

-        Passionate

Every employer is drawn to an employee who is always willing to do more than just what is required of him or her and that means getting involved in things that are not in his or her line of duty. This is the kind of person who continually surpasses expectations and gladly accepts any task or project, however challenging it may be.

Furthermore, a passionate person will not feel like he or she is working because they love what they do. The time he or she spends at work with his or her colleagues and superiors is so fulfilling to him or her.

Despite money being a motivator, people working for you should enjoy what they do to get paid. There are two questions that you can ask in an interview to identify if the candidate is a passionate person:

- At your last place of employment, what was it about your work that made you feel the most satisfied?

The candidate's answer to this question will tell you if the person is looking to apply his or her passion into his or her work or just looking for a comfortable workplace.

- How do you stay informed about your industry?

As far as passion is concerned, it will definitely be a red flag if the candidate cannot mention any recent development he or she has done whether positive or negative. Passionate people spend any extra time they have sharpening their skills and acquiring new knowledge. The genuine candidate will have enthusiasm showing in his or her eyes.

-          Reliable

There aren't many things that are more irritating to deal with than an employee who does not follow instructions. It shows that either he or she is not serious or fails to listen to instructions attentively.

The obvious result of such behavior is making mistakes, not meeting deadlines, faulty products, and disappointed or unhappy clients. An employee who does not listen until the entire instructions are given and also keeps interrupting shows a lack of respect to his boss.

By following instructions an employee shows that he takes his work seriously and is even capable of taking up extra responsibility. Additionally, a reliable employee will show up to work on time, inform the relevant authorities if he cannot make it and meets deadlines.

This type of employee has a greater chance to stick around the company for a while.

-          Positive

Most people do not like being around those who are negative, pessimistic or just unhappy. One should always be optimistic and happy no matter what they are going through.

Happiness and positivity are infectious hence the workplace will be full of happy people. Regardless of how monotonous or menial the given task is, a positive person will perform his or her duties happily and efficiently.

Additionally, employers feel good when they can identify problems and are willing to offer solutions. The more problem-solving skills they prove to have, the more valuable they are to the company. This kind of employee will bring you closer to realizing your company's goals.

To identify a positive candidate during the interview, you should ask questions like:

With examples can you mention one or two things that you are optimistic about in life?

-        Culturally fit

It can be difficult to find a candidate that matches your company's culture. To ensure that you get the best fit, first start by having a clear idea of your company's culture. Think about the values and characteristics of potential employees that you may hire and see if it lines up with you and your company's values. To find a candidate that fits into your company culture, you could ask any of the following questions:

-        With examples name three of your work-related values.

- Have ever made a mistake? If yes tell us how you fixed the problem.

When you find a candidate who is a match for your company culture, you should ensure that you offer them lucrative compensation packages, motivating leadership opportunities or chances of having a direct role in projects.

- Self-motivated/ Driven

You will not have to push self-motivated people to get work done. They continually work hard and always produce outstanding work. You will not have to worry about wasted time or having a lazy worker with a self-driven employee. They encourage others to copy their example. They have a great return on investment as they do not require any additional rewards.

Self-motivated individuals know their purpose in life and they are always able to rise above problems, loss, adversity and momentary failure. They believe in themselves as well as others. They embody humility and laugh at themselves, take criticism positively and admit when they are wrong. They regularly keep updating their knowledge and are very determined.

- Enthusiastic

People who portray enthusiasm and energy every day have an advantage over their workmates who are not as enthusiastic hence they easily burn out. Employees eager with a lot of liveliness are always excited to learn new things and aim for greater success. They contribute to making the work environment enjoyable and unique to their workmates. They also create an environment where new ideas are born regularly.

-        Hardworking

The benefits of hard work are irreplaceable. Some people work hard for a few years then they lose the psyche. Some people who specifically work from 9 to 5 can't exactly be considered to be hard working in a certain sense.

These people typically won't stay late or go the extra mile to get the job done. They'll do the minimum that's required of them. Hiring result oriented and industrious employees can greatly change the overall effectiveness of an organization. Such employees constantly remind themselves and the company of how important it is to keep working hard.

-        Team spirit

Most companies work in teams. Not only is it vital to work well individually but also as a team member. Performing well in a team takes good social skills, patience, and tolerance. Team efforts come with various advantages like when more people are involved in a project the work gets done faster, employee relationships are improved. Team members learn from each other's feedback.

-      Self –managed

Employers do not like employees who have to be told what is expected of them but rather those who know what is expected of them and are willing to go the extra mile. Additionally, a self-managed employee is aware of their duties and roles needed to improve themselves.

This allows him or her to use his or her strengths and minimize his or her weaknesses. Most self-managed employees are also self-disciplined hence they will not waste work time on distractions like their cellphone or browsing the internet. This kind of employee is diligent, always punctual and does not take unnecessary breaks or procrastinate.

-      Proactive

There are those employees who are reactive and there are those who are proactive. The reactive employees are the ones who have to be told what to do, whereas the proactive employees will take the initiative of trying to be more productive by being innovative. A proactive person always thinks ahead and executes without waiting to be requested to do so. This kind of employee stands out and is easily noticeable.

Moreover, strive to hire those who are willing to show initiative and take chances. Taking chances, of course, has a possibility of failure but failure offers a learning experience from which success is achieved. These are the employees who demonstrate confidence and bring new ideas to the table. They are also the employees that generate the most money for your company.

- Marketable

The right employee should also be presentable to clients a.k.a. marketable. This employee should positively represent your company by painting a picture of its values to the clients.

By so doing he or she should be able to give potential clients the confidence

they need to feel good about working with your company. Additionally, this person should have a great personality and demonstrate professionalism.

- Detail-oriented

Paying great attention to detail is critical as it eliminates the likelihood of making any unnecessary mistakes. An employee who can pay attention to every detail is always proud of his or her work. He or she will apply more effort without taking minor details for granted.

- Autonomous

Autonomy means giving employees the freedom to plan their work and execute it their own way. An autonomous employee will be able to deliver without having to inquire about everything that needs to be done from you since you also have a lot of work.

This kind of employee does not need supervision and will always deliver on projects delegated to him or her since they are a good time manager and very productive.

-        Creative

Creative employees come up with great ideas since they try out new things and always think outside the box. They therefore help minimize redundancy and monotony of the job, which in turn increases the employees' productivity.

-   Honest

Apart from an employee having the rest of these good qualities, the most important quality is genuine and integrity.

Straightforward employees also attract customer relations hence more growth for your company as a result of customer satisfaction.

An honest employee is transparent, which enhances the company culture thereby making every employee in the workplace have a sense of joy. Moreover, you will appreciate having honest and humble people in your company's management.

- Communicator

It is of great value to have employees who are capable of communicating eloquently. Poor communication skills could be harmful to any organization. It also involves an employee knowing what to say, how to say it, when to say it and whom to say. Inappropriate or inaccurate communication among employees could lead to internal disputes or even create problems with clients.

- Has leadership qualities

An employee who portrays leadership has self-confidence. This person will also be successful with any given task. This is the person you could consider assigning some leadership role to in your company.

Best Ways to Encourage and Motivate Employees to Do a Good Job

As a new business owner, the most important aspects you need to focus on are maximizing profits and enhancing productivity to keep your business going. To achieve this, you need your team of employees to work efficiently. Motivated employees will always strive to perform better. The following are some of the ways you can motivate your employees:

1.   Communicate better

You mustn't overlook communication. Ensure that you communicate with your employees regularly and in person.

By doing so, you will make them feel valuable. One on one communication is also the best way to go when you want to express your gratitude for their great job.

Your employees should not have to learn about issues concerning the company through rumors. Thus, you must update them on any changes in the company. This will maintain the team spirit.

2.   Be an example

As their leader, you must portray a good example. Positivity and good moods are infectious and your employees will follow suit. You cannot expect them to be everything that you are not. Things like believing in them will, in turn, make them believe in themselves and thus they'll be more productive.

3.   Empower them

Allow your employees to contribute in terms of ideas. By giving them room to share their suggestions, it helps in improving performance.

It does not end at listening to their contribution but also considering their advice and implementing it. If you only ask and then fail to make use of their suggestions, they will stop sharing their views.

Ensure that you give them the authority to make decisions as long as they are not negative and align with the company's policy.

4.   Offer advancement opportunities

Knowing that they are working towards something better or greater keeps your employees more motivated. They will have much to work for if they believe there is an opportunity for advancement.

Nobody wants to remain stuck in their career. Offering your employees training will motivate them by acquiring skills to help them move up in their careers.

By equipping them for better opportunities, your company earns a good reputation and the title of one of the best companies to work in.

5.   Provide incentives

The best way of motivating employees is through incentives. You don't have to get expensive things but rather something that helps you to express your appreciation. For instance gift cards, movie tickets, an extra day off with pay, or even rewards such as bonuses are great examples of incentives. Motivation should not be a once in a while kind of thing—it should be consistent. Motivation is critical in keeping the best employees, otherwise you will be facing a high turnover rate.

CHAPTER 9: BUDGETING AND COMPETITION

Setting up a budget for your business is a necessity. Even large corporations have budgets. Budgets are simply smart. They keep you on track, ensure that you are clear on what funds are being distributed and where, and allow you to accommodate all of the expenses that go into running your business.

Even when you first launch your business, you should have a budget. Not only is this smart for you, but if you do decide to go with investors, they will want to see your budget as well. Keeping your budget simple yet effective is the best way to ensure that your funds will be adequately used. This also makes it easier for you to ensure that you have enough to actually cover the expenses of running your business.

Below are the steps you need to take to create an effective business budget.

Understand Budgeting Basics

Budgets are a necessary tool for businesses. It is important to understand how a budget works in business, as it is quite different from how a personal budget operates. Often, personal budgets come with a sustainable income that does not change too much. This means that your budget stays fairly fixed. However, when it comes to business, you generally intend on creating more sales on a monthly, quarterly, and yearly basis. For that reason, you need to understand how your business budget is unique.

A budget that is created for a business will accommodate anticipated revenues. These revenues are generally calculated on the previous year (and up to about three years) in business. However, since you are just starting, you will need to generate your calculations based on market research. This will be your best-educated guess, and should likely be conservative to refrain from overestimating and not quite reaching your expectations. It is better to underestimate what you will make and come out with more than it is to overestimate and realize less.

Familiarize Yourself with the Three Components: Sales, Total Costs, Profits

The next thing you need to do is familiarize yourself with the three primary components in a business budget. These include sales, total costs (or expenses), and profits. These are the three numbers you are primarily focusing on in your budget.

Here is the importance of each of these components and what you need to

know about them:

Sales

The sales number is generated by the amount of money your business makes. This includes all revenue streams, not just any particular level of sales. Any money coming into your business should go here. You should include your current position, as well as a forecast for your future projections. You will learn more about forecasting in a later section.

Total Costs

Your total costs account for all of the costs involved in the running of your business. This includes your overhead and everything you spend to actually get the sales coming into your business. You should include your fixed costs, such as rent, variable costs, such as the cost of materials needed to make your products, and the semi-variable costs, such as your employees' salaries.

Profits

Profit is the number you are left with when you calculate your revenue minus total costs. Profit is generally your business's goal, so you want to ensure that your total costs are low enough that there is actually a profit to be had. This ensures that you earn a decent return on your investment.

Forecast Your Revenue

Forecasting what your revenue will be in future months, quarters, and years takes some practice. Since you are likely brand new in business, or within your first year, there is a good chance that you do not already have a strong enough volume of existing revenue to help you generate a number that is accurate for your business. This means you will have to research what other young businesses in your industry are accomplishing and estimate what a reasonable number would be for you.

Remember, since this is a prediction or projection method and not set-in- stone, forecasts are rarely accurate. Instead, they simply provide a guideline for what to expect when it comes to running your business. This forecast will give you goals, milestones, and direction, but will likely need to be adjusted along the way to represent what is going on in your business.

The best way to forecast effectively is to be conservative. Remember, it is better to expect lesser results and achieve higher ones than it is to expect higher results and achieve lesser ones. You should assume that your sales

103

volume will be lower and that your total costs may be higher. This ensures that you are conservative and hedged against unexpected expenses or circumstances.

Create a Spreadsheet

Once you are ready to begin, you'll want to start by having a spreadsheet. You can use many templates online, which may be the best way to start if you are new to budgeting. Otherwise, you can set up a spreadsheet for yourself. Again, if you choose to create your own, the best way is to use an existing template and adjust it as needed.

Determine the Details

With your spreadsheet ready, it is time to start putting together your budget! Begin with your fixed costs. Again, this includes anything that you must pay for every month set at a fixed expense. Start here, because these are the ones where you know exactly what they cost, exactly when they will come due, and are easy to predict.

Next, you'll need to estimate your variable costs and place them into your budget. This includes anything that will shift from month to month, depending on your monthly business activities. For example, if you sell products, you will have higher variable costs in months where you sell more products. Therefore, if you anticipate selling more products in any given month, you will need to adjust the volume of these expenses accordingly. These are the expenses that cannot be accurately predicted, especially when you are new in business. Add these into your budget.

Lastly, estimate what your semi-variable costs are going to be. These expenses are generally a fixed component, but certain things can result in them changing. For example, say you pay an employee a salaried wage but you determine that they will get a raise or a bonus. This would make it a variable cost because it does change over time, even if not too terribly much. Add these into your spreadsheet.

The last part you need to account for is your goal for earnings. You do this by creating a desired profit margin. So, say your desired profit margin is 10%. Your goal would be to make 10% more than your business will be spending to ensure that you actually generate a profit each month.

Budget for Unexpected Expenses

Unexpected expenses are a natural part of the business. They happen all the time. Something unforeseen may occur, or an unexpected accident may happen, and before you know it more expenses are required. This is especially true in new businesses. Since you are new to your business, you likely do not know exactly what it will take to run it. You might have an idea, but you may not be entirely clear on all of the costs surrounding this idea. Furthermore, you may decide that you need assistance or want to hire help to get things moving along.

Having funds set aside for unexpected expenses is the best way to protect yourself and your business. This will prevent you from eating into your other expenses or cutting your budget in many different ways to make up for the unexpected. A good rule of thumb is to set aside a certain amount of funds in a savings account for your business each month. This will ensure that you can afford anything that may arise unexpectedly.

Cash Flow

As a new business, you may not be entirely sure what to expect for your incoming and outgoing expenses. These can change drastically over time, and can also be challenging to produce when you do not have existing data already available from previous sales and cash flow. In this chapter, you will learn about how you can easily manage cash flow in your new business.

Know When You Will Break Even

You must have a strong idea as to when you are going to break even in your business. This means the point at which your income will meet the same value as your expenses. Use this as your goal and create milestones to help you reach this goal. This ensures that your business will not be running too long in the red.

Monitor Your Cash flow Management Regularly

You must monitor your cash flow effectively. In the beginning, especially, you need to refrain from focusing too much on your profits. While you need to keep these in mind, using these as milestones will make it feel like you are forever failing at what you are trying to accomplish. Instead, focus on using these as your goals and create milestones to help you get there. Pay attention to passing these milestones, and the goals will be fulfilled naturally.

The more regularly you monitor your cash flow, the more you will determine where your strengths and weaknesses are and what you can do to better achieve your milestones. You should make a habit of checking on your cash flow every week to ensure that you are successfully moving forward. This will also help you catch any weaknesses, mistakes, or other potentially detrimental situations immediately, rather than waiting and catching them far too late.

Maintain a Cash Reserve

No matter how incredible your plan is, you will have expenses come up that were unexpected. As we discussed in budgeting, you need to have a strong cash reserve available if anything comes up that requires additional funds. Keeping your cash reserves full and accessible when your business is not generating as much cash as it normally does, or when unexpected expenses arise is invaluable. This means that you will be

able to afford these expenses in cash, rather than going into debt to make up for it. Whenever possible, you want to do everything in cash. This can be a major lifesaver for your business in the long run, especially in new businesses.

Look for Opportunities to Optimize Cashflow Management

It is generally not a great idea to manage the cash in your own business unless you absolutely have to. Having an accountant on hand can make it a lot easier and ensure that your management is optimal. However, since you are just starting it is likely that you will have to manage your own cash flow for a while. For that reason, you need to regularly look for opportunities to optimize your cash flow.

The best way to simplify this is generally to use an online or digital platform known for managing cash flow. There are many digital platforms which you can use that will allow you to input your budget, monitor incoming expenses, and keep everything organized and manageable. Using one of these can help optimize your cash flow management big-time!

Collect Receivables Immediately

Whenever you make an invoice, make it "due immediately." Ensure that you have net terms that limit it to being paid within 15 days or less. Ensuring that your receivables are paid immediately means that you are not chasing after people for money. Early on in business, many entrepreneurs make the mistake of making things too lenient for their clients. As a result, many get taken advantage of. As well, it is money you can rely on in value, but not in timing. This puts it as a disadvantage to your company.

Offer Discounts for Earlier Payments

A great way to ensure that your clients pay sooner is to have discounts for those who pay in full or pay right away. You can also include in the net terms that there will be penalties for those who pay later. This usually encourages people to pay sooner and means that you are protected if they do not. Considering these parts of the service agreement can greatly protect your own earnings in your business.

Extend Payables When You Can

Although you want your receivables to be received as soon as possible, it is a good idea to set up your payables with as long of a payment period as possible. This means that, if you do not have the cash to pay immediately, you have some extra time to sort it out. Doing this is a great

way to hedge your business against those tough months and make the start-up process easier – without going into unnecessary debt.

Only Spend on Essentials

You really need to ensure that you are only spending money on things that are essential to your business, especially when you are starting. When people are starting, something that often happens is that they try to apply all of the bells and whistles of a mature company to their brand-new company. As a result, they end up spending far more than they need to. Focus only on what you must spend *right now* to acquire and maintain clients, and keep it at that. Refrain from having any unnecessary expenses. Only add more when they become necessary and when it makes sense to your business's growth and scaling.

Be Conservative When Hiring

When you are hiring people, be conservative. Refrain from hiring anyone unnecessarily, particularly when you are first starting. This will ensure that you are not spending money on salaries that could otherwise be saved or spent on something more valuable to the business. This is not only true for start-ups, though. This is true for any business. Be cautious about whom you are hiring and why. You should only hire those who will be an asset to your business, and only when that exact type of asset is truly needed to scale or grow your business further.

Use Your Technology Wisely

Technology is extremely helpful in the management of cash flow. Pay attention to using your digital cash flow management system and make the most out of it. Also, make sure that you are regularly backing up your data and protected against potential file corruption or data loss or theft. This will ensure that you can easily access it and that you are not worried about the possibility of it disappearing at any given moment.

Analyzing Competition

The trucking industry is very competitive. Customers have the luxury of choosing what company they want to work with. In the face of competition, companies have to develop close ties with customers. But regardless of competition, the core qualities of a successful business still do apply. It is vital to see how you stack against other companies. In the trucking industry, aggressive marketing is embraced considering the steep competition. Look for the weaknesses of other companies and capitalize on them.

Price

Gather information about your competitor's pricing plans. Generally, there are industry limits, and you would not find a quote beneath a certain figure. No matter how desperate your company may be, you have to respect the industry by enforcing the limit as it makes no business sense to operate at a loss. However, some of your competitors may be greedy. In such cases, you are at liberty to offer their customers sweeter deals. In this situation, you may engage in direct marketing efforts to their customers and show them how much they would save if they took up your offer.

Quality

When it comes to selecting carriers, customers are spoilt for choice. So you cannot afford to provide poor services. Customers want to work with consistent carriers. In your marketing efforts, you might want to single out carriers whose services are poor and attract their customers. Now, what consists of poor services in the trucking industry?

- Failure to beat deadlines
- Lack of necessary paperwork
- Inexperienced and incompetent personnel
- Poor packaging and transportation

You should present your company as a provider of quality services and highlight the areas that your competitors are weak on.

Add-on services

Customers love working with shippers who throw value-adding services into the deal. Actually, it is one of the secrets of retaining your customers. Try to determine whether your competitors offer add-on services, like cargo segmentation and integrations, or just dump the cargo and race off to the next gig. Offering additional services is a clever marketing tactic that gives customers a reason to stick with your company. However, do not stretch yourself too much as additional services may be costly in monetary and time factors.

Inventory

Sometimes, customers may work with carriers who have limited resources. For instance, if the carrier does not have enough trucks, it may lead to a lot of time wastage, and it is bad for business. You might want to attract customers from other carriers and bring them to you by having a stable company. This indicates that your company has a sound financial platform and can deliver quality services. In an industry plagued with inferior services, customers give positive reactions to carriers that demonstrate excellence.

CHAPTER 10: BULDING A TRUCKING COMPANY BRAND

Branding and marketing your business is an essential part of running any business. As we move into the discussion of branding and marketing, we get away from all legalities and focus on what is generally considered the more fun part of business! Here, you are going to learn how you can develop your brand. Your brand is essentially the "image" of your business. It personifies it and gives it a true feeling, allowing your customers to feel like they are interacting with a sentient being instead of just a cash cow.

Your brand is where you get to be creative. You can bring your business to life, create an image for it, and make it a lot of fun. Here you get to bring your vision into a reality and express that vision to your clients. Branding is extremely important. So, let's take a look at what makes a brand! Knowledge of Target Audience

Strong brands have a powerful understanding of who their audience is. They know the exact demographic of who they are targeting, and as a result, they can create a powerful brand experience that appeals to their audience. Knowing your audience prevents you from attempting to create a brand that appeals to everyone. Since this is virtually impossible, unless you have a massive corporate brand like Walmart or Amazon, you will need to have a clear focus on who you are creating for.

Authenticity

Brand identities require authenticity. Attempting to create another run-of-the- mill brand image that has already been done a thousand times over will result in you not being seen or

112

experienced by your target audience. To put it simply, you bore them. Instead, you need to identify and understand why your brand is so different from other brands out there and what it is about you that attracts your audience. Keeping your brand authentic and unique means that you will stand apart from the rest of the crowd. It also ensures that you will be memorable, capturing and staying in the minds of your target audience long after they interact with your brand.

Passion

Brands that have a passion for what they are doing end up being the most successful brands. People love a brand that is personified. They want to emotionally resonate with the brands they love on a deep and intimate level.

By interacting with your audience through effective, passionate branding, you make it a lot easier for them to fall in love with you and enjoy your brand experience.

Consistency

If you expect to receive repeat sales and keep your business afloat and with a positive reputation, you need to take advantage of your business's power of consistency. Consistency allows you to ensure that your customers receive the same phenomenal experience every time they interact with your brand. As a result, they begin to recognize you as a reliable, high quality, and enjoyable brand to interact with. Make sure to create a high-quality customer experience that you can easily repeat every single time, so that your customers always enjoy interacting with your brand.

Competitiveness

As we move forward with the digital age, becoming an entrepreneur gets easier, more and more people are entering the business world. This means many different brands are being developed and shared with your target audience regularly. As a result, you need to consider your competitiveness. Competitiveness plays a large role in making your brand stand apart and developing one that is worth pursuing. If you want your audience to recognize you and not your competitor, you need to be ready to take on the role of being at the top of the food chain. Prepare yourself by being willing to be a mover and shaker and by doing things differently.

Exposure

Exposure refers to the amount of viewing time your audience spends interacting with your brand. The more others view you, the better. This means that your audience grows rapidly because you are taking full advantage of getting in front of as many different eyes as possible. Using the internet, even extremely small companies with minimal budgets can be seen by thousands, if not tens and hundreds of thousands of new eyes, every month. Pay attention to your exposure and do whatever you can within your means to maximize people's number with their eyes on you.

Leadership

Virtually every brand has a particularly influential leader behind it. In a large company, this individual tends to be the CEO. In a smaller company, it will be the owner—otherwise known as you. You must be a strong leader for your brand and that you provide a positive influence on your team. Being the leader means that you can stay focused and on track. This means that your entire brand will stay focused and on track. Everything should pass through you first, before reaching the eyes of anyone else. This will ensure that you can qualify everything that contributes to your branding as something that supports your company in its growth.

Branding is not a one-and-done thing. Although a lot of effort goes into creating the initial groundwork for a brand, an overall brand becomes a living entity. With all of the moving parts and elements to the brand, it is easy to see why your audience will develop a relationship with your brand as long as it is created effectively. You must understand how you can create a brand that will last long-term. In this chapter, we will explore what is involved in creating a lifelong brand that your audience will grow to know and love!

Keep Your Image Recognizable

A recognizable brand is one that has an easy time lasting through the ages. You want to make sure that your audience knows who you are and that you are recognizable. This means that your imagery, fonts, graphics, logos, colors, and other visual aids need to remain consistent. You should also retain a consistent tone of voice behind your brand. Another great tool to use is a key phrase or tagline, which quickly enters the minds of anyone who thinks about your business.

Beyond these basics, however, you need to ensure that you keep your presence consistent and powerful. Building steadily and with integrity along the same recognizable pattern means that your audience will always know exactly who they are looking for.

Stay Flexible and Be Open to Evolution

Brands evolve. Remember, they do eventually become an entity and stand on their own. So naturally, just like a true being would, brands will evolve. The evolution is necessary. You want your brand to evolve with the times and stay relevant to all that is going on in the modern world. If you want to support your brand's longevity, you have to make sure that you are allowing your brand to evolve.

The key to successful brand evolution is to ensure that the evolution is subtle and happens over time. A great example of this process is Coca-Cola. When people think of Coca-Cola, they typically think of a true red color, the classic white Coca-Cola logo, and the feel-good, relaxing energy that accompanies their branding. In general, the image seems pretty consistent and solid. However, if you look through the history of Coca-Cola, some notable changes took place over time. At one point, the brand colors, fonts, and logo even changed. As a result of consistent, subtle changes, they were able to evolve the brand to stay relevant and modern, without making such drastic changes that people were no longer able to recognize or identify the brand.

You need to incorporate this natural evolution process into your brand, as well. This does not mean that early on you need to begin shifting and changing your brand. Instead, it means that as your company continues to remain intact and your brand continues to grow, you make subtle changes that make it more appealing to your growing audience and community of supporters. As a result, it grows even more enjoyable but does not become unrecognizable at any one point.

Maintain Your Purpose

Regardless of how your brand evolves, you need to ensure that your purpose for being in business remains the same. You do not want to operate with one single purpose and use it to capture your audience's hearts, only to flip the switch and completely change it. Especially not over and over again. Keeping your purpose clear, focused, and consistent ensures that your audience knows exactly what you are about and why you are in business.

You can also use your purpose to enhance their emotions and inspire them to follow you even more. For example, consider IKEA. This is a furniture company whose purpose is to "create a better everyday life." Their furniture is designed to make it easy to assemble, while being attractive and highly functional for their clients. They use this to enhance their client's emotional desire to have ease and functionality as a staple in their life. Often, they incorporate their clients' emotions by showing them that this ease and functionality directly contributes to them having a more enjoyable family life. In their advertising you often see families gathering together and enjoying each other more, thanks to the time they have saved from having functional and attractive homes due to IKEA furniture.

Involve Your Employees

If you are a company with employees, or when you do begin to incorporate employees into your company, always take the time to bring your employees into the branding process. Your employees likely interact with your audience a lot, maybe even more than you do. As a result, it is important to consult them when it comes to branding. This does not necessarily mean that they get the final say. However, including their input and listening to their inspiration is a great way to magnify your brand's success.

Consider this: having several pairs of eyes focused on the success of your brand is powerful. This means having several different perspectives, insights, inspirations, and ideas to contribute to how you can evolve and expand your brand to become even more successful. You want to have several eyes on your brand, whenever possible. Your employees already work for you, and generally love being included in these types of processes. Incorporating your employees is a great way to enhance your brand's quality and make it more appealing to your audience.

Enhance Customer Loyalty

Rewarding loyal people to your brand is a great way to maintain their loyalty and turn them into lifelong fans. If you want to have a long- lasting brand, you need to recognize who your biggest fans are and show them gratitude for the support that they have offered your company throughout the years.

The customers who are loyal to you are the ones who consistently go out of their way to share about you. They write to you, or write reviews about you, they share you with their friends and family, and they otherwise rave about how awesome you are to work with, or how incredible your company is. These individuals share you a lot, which means you are receiving a lot of added business from them. Showing them thanks through exclusive rewards and perks is a great way to thank them for all that they do for you.

In some cases, simply offering a heartfelt thank you is enough. You may prefer to make it a little more tangible and offer discounts or free swag to these fans in other circumstances. Giving your biggest fans the star treatment is a great way to show them that you are just as grateful for them as they are for you, which further expands brand loyalty. When people see this type of back-and-forth exchange between companies, they become far more interested in what all of the love is about!

Be Aware of Your Competition

As with any aspect of your company, you need to be aware of your competition regarding your branding. Paying attention to what your competition is doing is a great way to enhance your strategy, learn from their successes and mistakes, and catapult yourself into further success. Ultimately, you can use this awareness to tailor your brand to fill the gaps that other brands are presently serving. The idea is to create a brand that appears and feels superior to the other brands out there. You want your customers to come to you, not to your competitor.

CHAPTER 11: COMMON MISTAKES

It's good to learn about the negatives before you indulge in the business and find yourself making the same mistakes. We'll go over some of the most common mistakes that beginners in the trucking business make.

The mistakes are so numerous that I can't exhaust them all here. The following should be of help to you as you start your journey in this industry. They include:

■   **Growing too fast**

As much as you want to see your business grow, it is important to ensure that you do not do it too fast lest you cause harm. For example, over-booking loads and missing ETA's because you didn't plan accordingly could negatively affect your reputation. Starting to employ people unnecessarily could lower your revenue since salaries are one of the most expensive costs of your operation

-   **DOT regulations**

The United States Department of Transportation is a federal body that regulates transportation affairs in the US. The body was created through an act of Congress and is governed by the secretary of transportation. The USDOT has various regulations to ensure that the transportation industry operates within the highest possible standards.

Drugs and Alcohol

Drugs and alcohol can lead to disasters on the roads. Drivers who are under the influence pose a risk to other road users. The United States Congress made a law in 1991 authorizing DOT agencies to take drug and alcohol tests on drivers. This program of conducting drug and alcohol tests is known as Part 40. The program is comprehensive and works for the good of the transportation industry.

Cell Phones

The DOT criminalized the use of cell phones by drivers while on the road. If a commercial driver is found using their phone while driving, they are slapped with a $2,750 fine. This law is endorsed by the Federal Motor Carrier Safety Administration (FMCSA) and the Pipeline and Hazardous Materials Safety Administration (PHMSA). This law is aimed at ensuring that drivers are laser-focused. When a driver takes their eyes off the road, they risk causing an accident.

Vehicle Safety Standards

The United States Department of Transportation requires vehicles to be well-equipped to guarantee safety on the road. Vehicles with missing or defective parts should not be brought to the road. Here are some of the safety guidelines:

Controls and Displays

This standard requires that motor vehicle controls and indicators are in great working condition, ensuring their visibility in daylight and night. This reduces safety hazards because drivers are less distracted.

Defrosting and Defogging of Windshield

This standard requires that every truck has defrosting and defogging systems on the windshield that either apply heat to the windshield or dehumidify the vehicle's air.

Windshield Washing System

The windshield washing system should be in good condition, so that it may keep the windows clear in rainy or snowy conditions, thus not sabotaging the driver's scope of vision.

Brake System

This standard requires that trucks should have their brakes in great working condition. Brakes are critical in most road emergencies, and if they were faulty, it could mean a disaster. The DOT requires that both hydraulic and electric brake systems are in great condition.

Reflective Devices and Associated Equipment

This standard aims to ensure adequate illumination of the road and ensure that trucks can be seen and that their signals are understood. Poor lamps, reflective devices, and other equipment may cause other drivers to have blurred vision that results in road accidents.

Tires

Trucks should have great tires. The tires should be optimized for resistance, endurance, strength, and speed. Balding and defective tires could cause the truck owner to be on the bad side of the law.

Rearview Mirrors

The driver is supposed to be alert about what is happening behind the truck as they are with what is ahead. That is why the driver needs rearview mirrors. The daring drivers who move around without rearview mirrors are not only risking their lives, but they could also be fined if found.

Hood Latch

The hood latch system is critical for road safety.

Theft Protection

This standard requires that every truck is fitted with a system of thwarting theft. There are many incidences of trucks getting stolen. Owners should acquire technologies that send out an alarm when an unauthorized person tries to drive off with the truck.

Accelerator Control System

Trucks are famous for their acceleration capabilities. But the truck's throttle is supposed to return to an idle position when the driver is no longer accelerating or when there is a disconnection in the control system.

Electronic Stability Control Systems

This standard aims to minimize fatalities from accidents in which drivers lose control and rollover. The electronic stability control systems are critical in the sense that they increase stability.

Driver's Impact Protection from the Steering Wheel System

The steering wheel can cause fatal impact, so the truck should be fitted with a system that protects the driver from the chest, neck, and facial injuries in an accident.

Glazing Materials Protection System

The purpose of this standard is to reduce injuries that originate from crashing into glazing materials.

Door Locks and Door Retention Components

The doors should be secured properly with strong latches, hinges, and other supporting material to eliminate the potential of occupants being ejected in the event of an impact.

Roof Crush Resistance

This standard ensures that the compartment is well-secured to protect the people inside the compartment during rollover accidents.

Rear Impact Guards

This standard lowers the number of fatalities and injuries when light duty cars crash into the truck's rear end.

Vehicle Identification Number Requirements

This standard is aimed at simplifying the retrieval of vehicle-identification information and their record.

- Not having enough insurance coverage

Most new entrants meet the basic guidelines of having liability and cargo insurance coverage. It's vital that you also get physical damage of non-owned trailer coverage and general liability coverage, protecting your driver and others if the truck is not involved.

Note that depending on your fleet size and type, workers compensation coverage may be needed as well. Make sure you understand all of your business needs and get the correct coverage based on that. A lack of proper insurance coverage has led to some trucking businesses being incapable of paying for damages.

- Not understanding your true cost per mile

As discussed earlier you must understand both your businesses' fixed costs and variable costs. Just as a reminder, fixed costs are expenses automatically incurred whether your truck is running or parked.

An example of fixed costs would include things like insurance and rent. Variable costs are the unpredictable costs such as truck maintenance and fuel costs.

When you're starting your business you should have enough cash to cover your business expenses for 3 to 6 months since you'll need to cover these costs before your business starts earning any money. Keep in mind that it's not a guarantee that your business will grow as fast as you expect in the beginning. To manage your cash flow, it's important that you know the right cost per mile.

Your other business financial reports and the cost per mile are measuring your business' financial health. You should understand your basic cost per mile based on the annual expenses of your trucks and their annual mileage. This can be achieved by dividing the annual costs by the number of miles covered that year. The challenge, however, is allocating all the expenses accurately. This is the main reason most businesses don't survive. Most new trucking businesses fail to take the time to understand their cost per mile, their expenses, and how to document these expenses. Also, they accept almost any rate offered just to get a load. Before they know it, they encounter problems with their cash flow. This means that they become unable to pay their bills, drivers are not making them enough money, and eventually the business starts crumbling.

-   Being cheap about marketing

Most new trucking businesses do not understand the magnitude of promoting and marketing their business. Most new ventures think that word of mouth and a few fliers will do, but this isn't always the case.

Your marketing strategy will determine whether your business sinks or floats.

Marketing, just like other factors involved requires strategic planning.

Start by identifying the area that you want your business to cover and research prospective customers. Then decide on the media you'll employ, including opening a page on social media and being active.

This will help to create awareness. You can also create memorable and relevant business cards, make posters, get ad space in your local business magazine or newspaper, etc. Marketing is the backbone of every business and it's where you'll get most of your leads.

Ensure that you allocate enough resources for marketing. In the beginning, it will be costlier but once your business gains ground, you will have established your brand and ultimately realize that marketing pays off.

- ## Hiring the wrong employees

Hiring employees is not an easy task and it should involve a thorough process as discussed earlier. This is possible by first identifying what it is that your business needs. This is also in line with whether you need employees. As we pointed out earlier, hiring unnecessarily will just increase your salary costs and eat into your revenue. You should consider outsourcing certain tasks when needed as a cheaper alternative.

- ## Lack of a clear written plan

It's paramount that you have a clear plan for your business and it should be written. The goals should be achievable and relevant. Aim to also have an inspiring vision for your business because your mission will make it possible to achieve your vision in the future. Lacking a good plan has led to most startups getting stuck along the way. Some to the extent of shutting down because they did not put much thought into their business plan.

- ## Listening to family and friends

I know this sounds weird because these are the people you trust the most. However, they may be lacking the experience needed to run a trucking business, yet they want to give you advice on the topic. Take their advice with a grain of salt if they don't have any experience in the industry. You wouldn't take financial advice from someone who's broke and the same premise applies here.

- Unexpected expenses

Most new owner-operators are under the assumption that just because they purchased a brand-new truck, there will be no need for maintenance costs or costs incurred due to the truck breaking down. They end up eliminating this cost while budgeting hence affecting their business revenue.

- Assuming there will always be work

Most new trucking business ventures live under the illusion that they will always be busy once they start the company. The reality is that it will take time to build up a client list and it requires a lot of patience and persistence to get your business to a high-income level.

CHAPTER 12: BOOKEEPING

Bookkeeping is an essential, yet sometimes confusing part of the business. This is especially true for new businesses. Mature businesses typically have the luxury of hiring an official bookkeeper. Still, as a start-up, it is likely easier for you to learn how to do this yourself so that you can allot finances to more growth-focused areas of your business.

In this chapter, we will explore what you need to do to keep your bookkeeping duties simple yet efficient. This will be extremely helpful for managing accounts, overlooking cash flow, paying taxes, and more. Even if you don't necessarily want to, make sure that you start this immediately. This will save you from being disorganized and frustrated later on.

Keep Your Business and Personal Finances Separate

If you are running a sole proprietorship, or are running an LLC by yourself, it may seem like the easiest solution is to run your accounts together. The truth is, this is actually not effective and not ideal.

One major thing here is that your tax auditor can audit both you and your business when it comes to tax season if you keep your finances together. This can be extremely frustrating for everyone involved. So, the better choice is to keep them separate from the very beginning. Treat your business as its own entity, even if it technically is not one.

A great way to keep them separate is to have your payments go into a bank account made specifically for your business. You can then have your business pay you on set days each month, just like a regular paycheck. Your business can then be run on the remaining funds. You are paid first and receive funds, but everything is being operated effectively and separately.

File Your Tax Compliance Reports on Time

If you do not file your taxes on time, you can end up paying some major penalties. Even if you will not pay the entire balance due right away, you need to make sure you are on time. This can end up costing you big money if you aren't.

A great way to manage your tax funds is to have a separate account open and automatically transfer a certain amount into that account every time your business receives money. This way, you have all of the funds you need to pay

your taxes when tax season rolls around.

Keep Organized

There is nothing worse than having your bookkeeping systems messy and not finding what you need. Should you get audited or otherwise need to have access to certain information, not locating it can result in serious penalties. You want to make sure that you are filing on time, and that everything is kept organized. Not only will this make taxes themselves easier, but it will also make managing and monitoring your money, overseeing your accounts, etc., easier to stay on top of.

A great way to keep things organized is to start by having an effective method that you will use to handle all of the paperwork that comes through. Most people will use a basic filing system that keeps everything organized by purpose, category, and otherwise. Pick a system that works for you and stick to it. This will ensure that you know exactly where to look to find everything that you need.

You should also enter your bookkeeping data in batches. Have a set date each month or week where all of your information is inputted into an online organizational platform. This way you have the hard copies available in your paperwork filing, but you also have everything backed up and organized online, too.

Another thing you need to do is continually pay attention to managing your cash flow. You want to stay on top of where money is coming from, and where it is going. Doing this will ensure that you are clear on what you are spending and what you are receiving. Regularly overlooking this can also ensure that you can correct this issue immediately and protect yourself from unnecessary financial loss if you are wasting or overspending in any particular area.

Lastly, you need to review your bank statement and financial reports every month. This will ensure that everything you have stored in your bookkeeping records is accurate and that nothing has been missed. It is a lot easier to catch a potential mistake right away and correct it than wait several months and have no idea where the mistake was made, or what it was. As well, in many cases, if you wait too long, it cannot be corrected. Staying on top of this will keep everything organized and accurate.

Audit-Proof Your Records

If you are audited, you will want to ensure that you have everything available for the auditors. For that reason, it is better to audit- proof your own records. Or, audit yourself. When you do this, you will ensure that anything an auditor may ask for or need to see is readily available for you.

To audit-proof yourself and your records, you need to ensure that you keep all of your debit and credit receipts. Any time you receive one, no matter how small the receipt is, keep it and file it under the category it belongs to. This way, if anyone ever needs them, you have them available and organized.

You should also ensure that you deposit all of your business cash flowing into the business. This will ensure that you can prove taxable (income) and what is not taxable (loans). This is a part of ensuring that you will not seem as though you are evading taxes for any given reason, or otherwise wrongfully structuring your tax returns.

Whenever Possible, Don't Go Into Debt

Lastly, the best thing you can do is run your business on any cash already coming into your business. If you do not have enough funds to cover all of your expenses, you should consider how expenses can be cut. A great idea is to ensure that you do not offer credit or otherwise to your customers, as you are not a bank, not your responsibility.

Whenever you can avoid going into debt, do so. Going into debt can make bookkeeping a lot more challenging. The more straightforward you can keep it, especially when you are newer and unsure as to exactly what you are doing, the easier it will be for you to use it.

CHAPTER 13: AUTOMATION AND SECRET TIPS

Automation is a highly popularized tool for scaling businesses in the modern world, and great reason. When it comes to scaling, automation is extremely powerful. However, there is a lot of false information going around about the purpose and use of scaling, and when, how, and why you should do it. In this chapter, we will explore this valuable tool and discover how it will benefit you and how you know it is the right time to start using it.

Why Waiting Is Better

Many get-rich-quick schemes out there advertise that starting and running a fully-automated business is the way to make money in your sleep right off the bat. Unfortunately, the only people who tend to get rich from these systems are selling you the automated services. In the past, this may have worked, but people want a relationship with the company they are purchasing from in modern times. Therefore, most fully automated businesses, especially ones that are brand new, tend to be overlooked and unappreciated by your target audience.

Instead of causing a gap in your relationship with your audience, you should consider waiting and not implementing automation until later (see: "When to Start" below). Waiting gives you plenty of time to develop genuine, personalized connections with your audience. This means that they truly get to know who you are and what your brand is all about. Furthermore, it allows you to create market research. You begin to understand who your audience is, how they communicate, what they love about your business, and why they are actually interested in it.

When to Start

Knowing when to start automation is simple: you start when adding massive value to your customer relationships. Keep in mind that automation tends to be considered "impersonal." Therefore, you need to build a highly personalized brand that is great at creating genuine relationships. Then, once you have done so, you can use these automation tools to amplify your clients' value and further improve your relationships.

For example, say you spend the first six months of your business building relationships through personal connections. You network, offer free live training, input your inspired written content and so forth during this time.

Then, at some point, you realize your relationships are growing and it is taking up far too much time for you to continue to nurture them exclusively in this way. So, instead of carrying on and putting too much on your plate and burning out, you begin to download some of your live training and automate them. You include them on a landing page with a sign-up link. This allows your audience to establish a personal connection with you through email and gives them access to the free live training. That way, they gain access to the added value that you have already given away for free. However, they also gain the opportunity to build a personal connection with you through your e-mail newsletter.

The only time you should truly implement automation is when you have scaled through personal interaction enough to become too much. When you no longer feel like you have adequate time to devote personal one- on-one attention, you begin including automated content and sources. This way, you can still include some personalized content, but you are not strapped down to your computer 24/7 trying to keep up with all of the relationships you have created with your clients.

How Automation Will Benefit You

Once you are ready to begin automating your business, the benefit you gain is massive. It makes building and scaling your business significantly easier. Because you can automate things, you can create a single piece of content and use it several times to establish new customer relationships and provide added value to existing ones.

Another great automation tool is using automated post schedulers to post all of your content for you. Then, instead of having to jump on your computer or phone daily and upload new content, you can simply schedule it out for several days or even weeks in advance. This allows you to spend more time away from your computer and business creating more inspired content or enjoying your life, rather than feeling hung up having to personally be involved in every little detail.

At the end of the day, the most important thing is that your business makes a profit, and it doesn't hurt to extend your profit margins. Everyone pretty much knows the habits that will help you increase your profits. It is the usual stuff: be punctual, handle your paperwork, take care of your customers, and reward your drivers.

However, these are the not-so-known secrets of increasing the profits of your trucking business:

Outsource the dispatch department

The dispatch department ensures that the orders are matched with the appropriate driver. They play a vital role in the trucking industry. However, the dispatchers can be quite expensive in the United States, and their average cost is $1,400 per week. You may work around this by outsourcing your dispatchers to Europe. It is a great cost-reduction measure considering that it would cost $400 per week.

Use fuel cards

A fuel card is an effective way of easing your paperwork, and it eases the process of tracking your expenses. Fuel cards also make much economic sense because they entitle the user to discounts and rebates. The discounts might seem small at first, but these little amounts eventually add up to quite a substantial amount. Fuel cards also offer critical safety measures, as the driver no longer has to move around with cash which can make him a target. Considering that you can impose limits on the type of transactions you can have with a fuel card, this goes a long way in managing expenses.

Seek freight factoring deals

Freight factoring, also known as trucking factoring, is an arrangement where trucking companies sell their accounts receivable to a factoring company. Considering that payments are made long after carriers have made the delivery, an owner-operator may be in cash straits. The owner-operator may decide to sell their invoice to a factoring company who will eventually get paid by the customer. Upon submitting the invoice, the owner-operator receives an advance that the balance will be cleared later when the customer pays. This is a great method of ensuring the normal operations of your business.

Secure a great deal for your trucking company insurance

For one, the trucking business can be very risky. What would happen if you hired a junkie and they went out and crashed your truck? If you don't have the right insurance cover, it could mean a financial disaster. Go through the policies, be informed, and resist making decisions based on your emotions alone. Having a great insurance coverage will boost client confidence. Considering that regular shippers want to work with carriers who are serious about insurance, it could mean more business for you.

Install GPS on trucks

Installing GPS on your fleet is a major step forward. Thanks to GPS, you can stop calling drivers now and then ask where they are which is painfully annoying. You can always check up on where they are without interrupting them with never-ending calls. You can also keep concerned customers updated on the progress of their cargos and help them estimate the time their load arrives. In the unfortunate instance that the truck is stolen, it would be very easy to locate it especially by following the GPS signal. Also, GPS sends automatic alerts when the truck leaves without authorization. Having GPS makes economic sense because it saves you from troubles that would have otherwise cost you a lot.

Install fuel theft prevention systems

You would be surprised to know that fuel theft is more common than people think. It is estimated that an average truck may lose up to $1,000 worth of fuel to thieves every month, and that is a shocking figure! To protect yourself against being set back $1,000 every month, you may want to fit a fuel theft prevention system.

Purchase maintenance plan (Penske, Ryder)

This is a great tactic of reducing maintenance expenses.

Give drivers specialized training

Train and educate drivers on safe driving. Make them drop unhealthy habits like dividing their attention while driving. Great drivers are the biggest investment of a trucking company.

They are the force behind a growing trucking company. One of the reasons that contribute to a high turnover of drivers in trucking companies is the loss of respect. When you train your drivers, it is actually a show of respect, and you are more likely to retain them.

Use cloud-based software for management purposes

Powerful trucking management software simplifies things. It can help you

handle mind-numbing paperwork. You can use the software to perform accounting tasks, create invoices, and send the invoices to your debtors. Trucking management software helps you to manage fleets; if you approached each truck at a time, it would be incredibly monotonous and tiresome. Management software improves data accuracy, decreases inventory costs, and extends the profit margins.

CONCLUSION

Starting a trucking business is a massive undertaking. As a new business owner, you are taking on a lot of roles and responsibilities at once. Especially in the very beginning, virtually everything that goes into running your business will fall on your own shoulders, and if applicable, your partners'. This means that you need to be prepared to handle all that comes with this commitment and educate yourself in every way possible.

While you don't need to make it more complicated than it already is, you need to understand that it *is* a complicated task and require your devotion and commitment.

However, one wonderful thing about business is that there is nothing more fulfilling than seeing a vision that you are deeply passionate about coming to life. As long as you have a strong strategy in place and the willingness to overcome any obstacle that lands in your path, you are sure to experience success in your entrepreneurial journey.

The trucking industry is still a promising industry with many opportunities for those interested in getting started. Like starting any other business, it will require patience, perseverance, and an urge to learn.

Through reading this book, I hope that you were able to learn plenty of information to help you get started on that path. From developing your idea to knowing how and when to scale it, I have done my best to include as much information in this book as I could to help you get started.